Not a Living Breathing Document:
Reclaiming our Constitution

An Introduction to

the Historic Foundations

of American Liberty

By KrisAnne Hall

John Adams on the Constitution:

I read it with great satisfaction, as the result of good heads prompted by good hearts, as an experiment better adapted to the genius, character, situation, and relations of this nation and country than any which had ever been proposed or suggested. In its general principles and great outlines it was conformable to such a system of government as I had ever most esteemed... It was not then, nor has been since, any objection to it in my mind...Nor have I ever entertained a thought of promoting any alteration in it but such as the people themselves, in the course of their experience, should see and feel to be necessary or expedient, and by their representatives in Congress and the State legislatures, according to the Constitution itself, adopt and ordain.

Inaugural Address, 1797

Table of Contents

Content   **page**

Foreword

KrisAnne Hall was born and raised in St. Louis, MO. The daughter of a sheet metal worker, she learned early the value of hard work and patriotism. In 1991 she worked her way through Blackburn College in Carlinville, IL and graduated with a bachelor's degree in Bio-Chemistry.

In 1996 KrisAnne enlisted in the US Army and was trained as a Russian Linguist at the Defense Language Institute in beautiful Monterey, California. It was there she met her husband, a Russian language instructor in the US Navy. After a traumatic injury that led to a total hip replacement, she was honorably discharged with a service connected disability and moved to North Florida.

KrisAnne received her Juris Doctorate from the University of Florida, Levin College of Law in 2003. Before she graduated from law school, she began working for the State Attorney's Office in the Third Judicial Circuit of Florida as a certified legal intern; by the time she graduated she already had 10 jury trials under her belt. Upon graduation she continued to work as a prosecutor saying she *"enjoyed wearing the white hat."* KrisAnne says she has *"always had a heart to serve people,"* and as a prosecutor she felt like she was serving her *"community and the people of Florida."*

In 2006 KrisAnne and her husband adopted their son, Colton. In June 2007 her servant's heart and an opportunity to spend more time at home with her son, drew her into another arena – Constitutional Law. She left the State Attorney's Office to work for the Gibbs Law Firm, a Constitutional Law Firm, representing the first amendment rights of religious liberty and free speech. She defended churches, preachers, Christian schools and individual Christians and their First Amendment rights - not realizing that God was preparing her for her own first amendment battle.

In July of 2009 she returned to the State Attorney's Office where her boss Mr. Jerry Blair had been replaced by Mr. Robert "Skip" Jarvis, a former co-worker. While working at the SAO, KrisAnne earned the respect of Law Enforcement, Public Defender's Office, Judges and community leaders. She distinguished herself as a top-notch prosecutor (attested to even by Mr. Jarvis).

At the end of January, due to her background with the Constitutional Law firm, KrisAnne was asked by the Chairman of the Suwannee REC to help review a Constitutional primer he was to give to voters in Dowling Park, Florida. She was then asked by the Suwannee County Republican Executive Committee to give a presentation of her own on the Constitution. The presentation, on Constitutional Originalism was well-received and multiple invitations came in from various groups. She also taught the Constitution in the public school as a volunteer in Florida Supreme Court Justice, Fred Lewis' *"Justice Teaching"* program.

After giving many presentations over a period of four months with no complaint from her boss, KrisAnne received an invitation to speak on Constitutional issues at a tax day rally hosted by a local TEA Party. It was the speech at this gathering and an appearance on WJTK Radio program, explaining Attorney General Bill McCollum's lawsuit against the *Affordable Healthcare Act* that apparently invoked the wrath of her employer, Mr. Jarvis.

Mr. Jarvis contacted KrisAnne; and, said that he had received a complaint that one of his ASA's was using his office to "legitimize right wing fringe groups" Mr. Jarvis suggested that "discussing a desire for less government and smaller budgets" was an ethical violation, as it meant advocating against the State of Florida. Coincidentally, this was the very platform that our Governor was running on for his reelection. KrisAnne was further instructed by Mr. Jarvis that she must "disassociate herself" from these right wing fringe groups.

Having represented numerous first amendment issues, KrisAnne had become intimately acquainted with the abuses by those in power. She had watched as many of her clients at the Gibbs Law firm had been bullied and harassed. She also recognized what was at stake – surrender your rights and keep your job or take a stand and be fired. KrisAnne chose the latter, saying "Mr. Jarvis did not give me my rights, they are a gift from God, and I will not surrender them for a paycheck." On May 21, 2010 Mr. Jarvis fired KrisAnne for educating the public about our founding documents.

She now travels throughout the country teaching citizens the history of our founding documents and the principles of liberty contained in those documents. KrisAnne speaks with great passion and can maintain the attention of an audience for hours at a time. Her love for her country and its history is obvious to all who hear her. But she says her greatest passions are serving God and being a mother to a wonderful little boy. KrisAnne says, "being able to get our son Colton from birth and rescue him from the uncertain life he was headed for, has been one of the greatest blessings God has given me." This is the reason KrisAnne will not back down from what she believes is the calling of our generation – to reclaim the heritage of liberty bought and paid for with the blood of patriots "for the millions yet unborn."

-Chris Hall

Colton, Chris, KrisAnne

Doc Washburn (94.5 WFLA) and KrisAnne

8/28 Restoring Honor Rally

Frantz Kebreau and KrisAnne, GOTV Rally Middleburg

Herman Cain and KrisAnne, GOTV Rally Middleburg

Colton and Smokey

Building at Lowes

"When the past no longer illuminates the future,
the spirit walks in darkness."

-Alexis de Tocqueville

"As the British Constitution is the most subtle organism which has proceeded from the womb and long gestation of progressive history, so the American Constitution is, so far as I can see, the most wonderful work ever struck off at a given time by the brain and purpose of man."
— **W. E. Gladstone**

Preface

America is the land of opportunity. While no one is guaranteed success, no other nation on the planet gives a person greater access to what is needed to fulfill their dream than America gives to her citizens. I believe that America has a heritage of greatness; but, if we do not know where we came from and why, then we can lose the opportunity to be great. I hope this little book will inspire the readers to lay hold on that heritage. By realizing the solid foundations that make America exceptional, we can MAKE AMERICA GREAT ONCE AGAIN.

I also hope for this book to become a framework of history that we teach our children. Let's face it, there are some people we probably cannot reach – we must now look to our future; but, that future must be illuminated by the past. Hamilton and Madison in Federalist Paper No. 20 said, *"Experience is the oracle of truth; and where its responses are unequivocal, they should be conclusive and sacred."*

This book is based on the introduction to a series I teach on the Bill of Rights. It is an introduction to the roots of liberty which led to our great founding documents. I say introduction because it is just that, a beginning - an attempt to give the citizen a proper perspective and a starting reference to make further investigation into the roots of American liberty.

I also hope to give the reader a historical perspective to help refute the notion that the Constitution is a living, breathing document which must be interpreted and reinterpreted according to the changing needs of society. On the contrary, the meaning of our founding documents is firmly rooted in a long and detailed history. They embody a wisdom that was hard-earned through centuries of struggle for greater liberty.

In truth, the Declaration, the Bill of Rights and the Constitution are not documents born out of revolution, but rather out of "evolution." They were not created on a whim, so they should not be ignored and dismissed as the experimental dreams of a few rich, Anglo-Saxon, land owners. However, if we continue to accept the interpretation of those who would attempt to revise and conceal history, our great founding documents will be gradually destroyed and rendered powerless. For two and a half centuries we have lived under their protection -now they need our protection.

In the following pages I hope to acquaint the reader with a bit of history that needs to be reintroduced, first and foremost, into our homes and certainly into our schools, but especially into the halls of government. If we are to reclaim America's exceptionalism, then we must reclaim her history.

-KrisAnne Hall

P.S. I have left space throughout for notes. Don't just read this book – use it!

"Be not afraid of greatness;

some are born great,

some achieve greatness,

and others have greatness thrust upon them."

William Shakespeare

Ordinary Heroes

-

America's Founders

America Needs Ordinary Heroes

Do you ever marvel at the **bravery** and apparent genius of America's founders? I remember when I first discovered our founders in the book Founding Brothers, by Joseph Ellis. I wondered, "**How were these men able to dare and accomplish such a great feat as the establishment of the American republic?**" I was convinced that no men like these had ever lived or ever would again!

It is hard for me to consider the Constitution without a feeling of awe. Can you imagine being the author of the Declaration of Independence, the Bill of Rights or the Constitution? Seriously, who thinks "Yeah, I could've come up with all that?" How in the world did our founding fathers give us the greatest documents upon which any nation has ever been founded?

Just the preamble to the Declaration is enough to stir the heart of the patriot:

When, in the course of human events, it becomes necessary for one people to dissolve the political bands which have connected them with another, and to assume among the powers of the earth, the separate and equal station to which the laws of nature and of nature's God entitle them, a decent respect to the opinions of mankind requires that they should declare the causes which impel them to the separation.

We hold these truths to be self-evident, that all men are created equal, that they are endowed by their Creator with certain unalienable rights, that among these are life, liberty and the pursuit of happiness.

That to secure these rights, governments are instituted among men, deriving their just powers from the consent of the governed. That whenever any form of government becomes destructive to these ends, it is the right of the people to alter or to abolish it, and to institute new government, laying its foundation on such principles and organizing its powers in such form, as to them shall seem most likely to effect their safety and happiness.

Prudence, indeed, will dictate that governments long established should not be changed for light and transient causes; and accordingly all experience hath shown that mankind are more disposed to suffer, while evils are sufferable, than to right themselves by abolishing the forms to which they are accustomed. But when a long train of abuses and usurpations, pursuing invariably the same object evinces a design to reduce them under absolute despotism, it is their right, it is their duty, to throw off such government, and to provide new guards for their future security. -- Such has been the patient sufferance of these colonies; and such is now the necessity which constrains them to alter their former systems of government. The history of the present King of Great Britain is a history of repeated injuries and usurpations, all having in direct object the establishment of an absolute tyranny over these states.

What boldness!

What love!

Thank you God, for these men!

Just think about it - this small handful of brave colonists

 declaring war on the greatest military might on the planet! ...these courageous British subjects separating themselves from centuries of kingly rule and establishing for themselves and their descendants the **greatest representative government the world has ever known!**

Can you see yourself waking up one day and making those decisions? Do we see that kind of bold leadership today? Sometimes it's hard to think of very many great leaders in our nation today. We can probably name several charismatic politicians, but great leaders...not so much.

So then, why in colonial America was there such a preponderance of apparent visionaries? What made that time different from today? Surely we can list some examples of singularly great men at different moments of time; but, the generation of Americans in the 1700's seems uniquely exceptional.

You probably recognize some names of many of our founding fathers from that time - George Washington, Benjamin Franklin, Thomas Jefferson, Thomas Payne, Samuel Adams, James Madison, John Jay, Patrick Henry, Alexander Hamilton, John Hancock, Paul Revere.

You may even know some of the forgotten founders – James Otis Jr., Richard Henry Lee, Payton Randolph, John Leland, Henry Milton, Robert Morris, Edmund Jennings Randolph.

You may even be one the few who knows some of the heroines of Revolutionary America like Molly Hays McCauley, Penelope Barker, Elizabeth King, Mercy Otis Warren, Esther Reed, or Abigail Adams.

There is no doubt that these men and women undertook and accomplished a monumental feat; but, were they really unique? Did they have the **courage gene**? The **brilliance gene**? Or were they just a bunch of rebels that **got lucky**?

What about **YOU**?

Do you ever wonder, "**COULD I EVER BE GREAT** like that?"

Do you ever look at your **SON or DAUGHTER** and think, "Could I be raising the next George Washington? The next Molly Pitcher?"

Some have said extraordinary circumstances make extraordinary men. But it seems that during the revolutionary period, that being extraordinary was, in fact, ordinary. There was no shortage, apparently, of capable and courageous visionaries.

Consider a few examples:

-The attorney **Patrick Henry**. His bold oratory at St.
Johns Church in Richmond, Virginia decisively stirred the
Virginia House of Burgesses to send troops into the
revolutionary war. It is astounding to note that Henry's
oratory was so intense and so stirring that the
hearers were almost incapable of not taking
action; however, most could never recall what
he actually said! They just knew what they
had to do and couldn't help but do it!
Thomas Jefferson said of Patrick Henry's hypnotic
vocalizations:

*"Although it was difficult, when [Henry] had spoken, to
tell what he had said, yet, while speaking, it always
seemed directly to the point. When he had spoken in
opposition to my opinion, had produced a great effect,
and I myself had been highly delighted and moved, I have
asked myself, when he ceased, 'What the devil has he
said?' and could never answer the inquiry."*[1]

Where is that principled passion today among our leaders, much less among our attorneys?!? Oh, that we could be inspired by the passion of principle and truth, rather than by empty promises and theatrical rhetoric!

-The great pamphleteer **Thomas Paine**, a tailor and journalist. Paine wrote the 48-page pamphlet *Common Sense*. Because of its treasonous argument for independence from Great Britain, *Common Sense* was signed simply "Written by an Englishman." This anonymous publication sold 120,000 copies in 3 months and a half-million in the first year. John Adams reportedly said, "Without the pen of the author of '*Common Sense*,' the sword of Washington would have been raised in vain.[2]

COMMON SENSE;

ADDRESSED TO THE

INHABITANTS

OF

AMERICA,

On the following interesting

-We certainly cannot forget the statesman **Samuel Adams**, perhaps the original "community organizer" and originator of the T.E.A Party (or was that Penelope Barker?). Samuel Adams believed the government to be violating the British Constitution in the colonies. First in 1764 then again in 1772 he and his colleagues used the Committees of Correspondence to help coordinate resistance. He used the committees to bring like-minded patriots together throughout the Thirteen Colonies. These resistance groups led to the formation of the Sons of Liberty and the famous Boston **Tea Party** of 1773 and eventually the American Revolution.

Sam Adams used the Committees of Correspondence to rally **opposition against issues of overreaching, tyrannical government** and devise **plans of action.** A total of about 7,000 to 8,000 Patriots in 11 colonies served on these committees, they became the leaders of the American resistance to British oppression, and largely determined the war effort at the **state and local level.** They **promoted patriotism** and self-reliance, as well as sound financial stewardship and moderation. The committees gradually extended their influence over many aspects of American public life. They identified those who were not supportive of America, got rid of disloyal officials, and helped topple the entire Imperial system in each colony. They eventually **supervised the elections** of provincial conventions, which took over the actual operation of colonial government.

-**Ladies,** How about Penelope Barker of Edenton, North Carolina? Fed up with British tyranny and taxation, she organized the Edenton Tea Party in 1774. In the home of her friend Elizabeth King, she and 50 other women signed a declaration and sent it to be published in a London newspaper. In part the declaration said:

"Maybe it has only been men who have protested the king up to now. That only means we women have taken too long to let our voices be heard. We are signing our names to a document, not hiding ourselves behind costumes like the men in Boston did at their tea party. The British will know who we are...We, the aforesaid Ladys will not promote ye wear of any manufacturer from England until such time that all acts which tend to enslave our Native country shall be repealed."[4]

Much like the liberal media of today these principled women were attacked and portrayed by the British as bad mothers and loose women. However, the colonists praised these ladies and the women of the colonies followed their lead and began boycotting British goods.

Is it possible that men and women like this are forever lost? We know for certain that history often repeats itself; and therefore, tyranny is always a threat to be guarded against. What if the time arises when we need such patriots again?

How were they able to give us the foundation we have today through our founding documents?

There are certainly many elements that contributed to our founders' phenomenal accomplishments, not the least of which was a powerful faith and reliance on the providence and provision of God. But true faith is not blind faith. Real faith is built upon a foundation of what the faithful believe to be time-tested Truth.

And that is what the founders had, Time-Tested Truth, or to put it simply,

–The EXPERIENCE of History –

Experience of their own and the experience from generations of like-minded, freedom-loving people that came before them. They knew where they came from and why. They knew what they believed and why.

The truth is - they didn't just wake up one day and decide to create the greatest nation in the world and then begin to make up its framework out of thin air. Our founders, like us, had a heritage of liberty and (unlike us) they weren't ignorant of that heritage.

They knew their heritage because they knew their history. Because they knew their history, our founders knew what worked and they knew what was right.

Knowing that they were standing on a solid foundation of what worked and what was right contributed to the courage and resolve with which they pursued the cause of Liberty. If you know that what you are doing is right, then you can dare to do what others fear – **boldly face insurmountable odds - even if you have to go it alone.** I would like to boldly assert that these were just ordinary people.

Ordinary people **just like you**...**just like us**.

But they had a firm grasp on something that we have let slip; namely, **the truth and experience of THEIR OWN HISTORY.** Because they had **not** lost sight of their past or their vision of a better future for their children, ordinary people became extraordinary heroes. I believe that America needs heroes today. Those heroes are you and I equipped with a firm grasp of our history. As a certain leader has said, "We are the ones we've been waiting for." Except we don't want to overturn the values of America, we want to reclaim what made America great from the beginning. We can only do that if we rediscover how we got here in the first place.

Patrick Henry said, **"I have but one lamp by which my feet are guided, and that is the lamp of experience. I know of no way of judging the future but by the past."** In St. John's Church before the Virginia Convention, he boldly proclaimed "I know not what course others may take, but as for me Give Me Liberty or Give Me Death!"

In response to Patrick Henry's speech it is reported that those in attendance began to shout in response "Give Me Liberty, or Give Me Death! ...Give Me Liberty, or Give Me Death!" The rest, as they say, is history!

The fact is – once you have the courage to go it alone (because you know that your faith is rooted in rock-solid truth) others will follow.

So in the face of modern attacks against our founding documents, we must be reacquainted with the history that gave us these documents. Only then can we take a stand with a firm understanding of why the rights laid out in them are so important and timely for every generation.

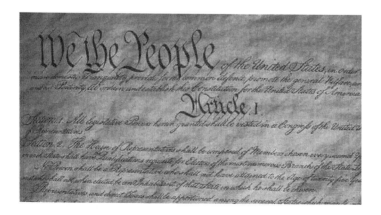

"The Constitution is not an instrument for the government to restrain the people; it is an instrument for the people to restrain the government - lest it come to dominate our lives and interests."
-**Patrick Henry**

Not a Living Breathing Document

Many like to assert that our Constitution is a living breathing document. The hidden meaning behind such language is the Constitution is outdated and does not or should not apply to modern society. It is a principle that allows its supporters to suggest scrapping the Constitution for some updated foreign or global system of law. This argument is disingenuous at best, since we have an amendment process built into the document itself that allows us to enact greater safeguards for the liberty of all Americans. Had the founders not included such a process we may still have slavery. The amendment process allows us to update the Constitution without scrapping its foundational principles. What sense would it make if just because you wanted to add an extra bathroom onto your house, you tear down the entire house? Our Constitution is amendable NOT a living, breathing document.

The first thing that we need to understand very clearly is that our founding documents were not created overnight. They were forged in the struggles for liberty for nearly over 700 years. While our Constitution may have been adopted in 1789 it did not originate in the 1700's. Its beginnings go back at least to the English Isles of 1066. While our heritage as individual Americans may not be English, the heritage of our founding documents is firmly rooted in English history. The men that laid the foundations of America were students of that history. When the abuses of King George III had reached a fevered pitch, America's residents recognized that they had been down this road before. They **didn't have to reinvent the wheel** – Oh, and by the way, **neither do we**. We just need to RECLAIM OUR HISTORY.

The Foundations of American Liberty

Our founding documents were not developed in the 1700's – their development began over 700 years earlier. Our founders were not creating new rights; they were asserting rights that they already enjoyed - rights that were being trampled by a tyrannical government. According to the principles of *Natural Law*, the founders believed that their rights came from God and that government had a duty to protect those rights.

It should be remembered that the American Revolution was not fought to throw off some foreign power. The inhabitants of America were British subjects. As Paul Revere road through the towns he cried "The *Regulars* are coming!" not the *British* are coming – he and his fellow citizens *were* British. The revolution was a fight to throw off the bonds of their own oppressive, overreaching government. For ten years the British subject of America endured the abuses of their king; and , when their petition went unheard – many of the citizens (like George Washington and Patrick Henry) decided enough was enough.

As the war for independence came to a close, a new government had to be established. That new government was established on principles and rights that the founding fathers already possessed.

Our founding documents' HISTORY alone should demonstrate that the Constitution and the Bill of Rights are not whimsical or malleable musings of a handful of revolutionaries. The development of our Bill of Rights and the formation of our Constitutional republic can be traced back for centuries.

Get ready to arm yourself with the truth. Don't just read the following sections – study them; research them for yourself. – Your children need you. The millions yet unborn are counting on you to arm yourself with the truth.

We do not need an armed revolution in the streets; we need **a revolution of the mind** - a revival of the heart of America and of her founding principles and of her history.

Here are the key building blocks in the evolution of our founding documents that each American citizen should know.

1066 William of Normandy

By 1066 England had one of the most complex governments in the medieval world. For at least 500 years England had been ruled by its King and to a large extent his council of advisers the Witan. The Witan consisted of the most powerful men in the land of both church and secular positions. While not always of a permanent character there is much evidence of charters and laws issued by this royal council. Clearly the seeds of parliamentary government go back at least to the Witan. England in 1066 was divided up into autonomous shires, each overseen by a "sheriff". This arrangement (which may have been passed down from the Roman Empire) sows the seeds of representative government in the hearts of the people, or more accurately stated, is a manifestation of their natural sense of liberty and independence.

England was unique in the medieval world in that the laws and directives were put in writing instead of being declared by word of mouth. Also, the governmental bodies were in fixed locations.

In 1066 William of Normandy conquers England, centralizes control of the shires and eliminates most of the ruling nobles, confiscates lands and institutes a heavy-handed rule. However, he does not completely dissolve that Anglo-Saxon style of government, but mixes it with Norman influence and creates a feudalistic nation. The Witan eventually concedes to his Kingship.

When his son William Rufus comes to the throne he continues to consolidate, but is detested by the people and poorly regarded by the church. Through a series of strange "accidents," Henry I takes the throne, and to gain favor after his brother's abuses, gives "concessions" to the people (nobles and barons) in the Charter of Liberties. This "written" mode of government sets the stage for the centuries-long process of "birthing" our Constitution.

1100 Charter of Liberties

In 1100 Henry I gained the throne of England; upon his accession he issued the 1100 Charter of Liberties. The Charter sought to make the **King subject to certain laws** regarding the treatment of church officials and nobles. The document addressed abuses of power by his predecessor, William Rufus (who had issued a charter in 1093 proclaiming the freedom of the people). The 1100 Charter reffered to the practices of William as – "oppressive and evil" – it addressed overtaxation, corruption and oppressive rule.

Here are two examples:

If any baron or earl of mine shall die, his heirs shall not be forced to purchase their inheritance, but shall retrieve it through force of law and custom

In other words - NO ESTATE TAX. In 1100 an estate tax or death tax was considered oppressive and evil. Somehow today your children don't deserve what you may leave them - but the government does ...?!?

If any of my barons commit a crime, he shall not bind himself to the crown with a payment as was done in the time of my father and brother, but shall stand for the crime as was custom and law before the time of my father, and make amends as are appropriate. Anyone guilty of treachery or other heinous crime shall make proper amends.

Translation: just because you are a member of government doesn't mean you are above the law. What a blessing it would be if our kingly rulers believed this today!

Although there is evidence that Henry ignored many of these promises, the Charter planted the seeds of liberty in the hearts of the people and continued to lay the legal foundation that would culminate in the creation of the US Constitution.

The Magna Carta of 1215

Although the 1100 Charter was ignored by most monarchs following Henry, it certainly did not escape the attention of the king's subjects. In 1213 Archbishop Stephen Langton, in the dispute between King John and Pope Innocent III, reminded the nobles that their liberties had been guaranteed over a century earlier **in the king's charter.** The present dispute was over King John's attempts to enter into matters of the Church. He attempted to appoint his own Archbishop overriding the election of Archbishop Langston. Archbishop Langston responded and John briefly yielded under the pressure of the Pope and declared that all rights protected **under the Charter of Liberties** should be observed.

The first of two councils lead by Langston was held simply to reassert the liberties contained in the 1100 Charter. At the second council a charter had been created that went even further in expanding the liberties that were to be protected. This became known as the Great Charter or Magna Carta, which Langston and the barons forced John to sign in 1215.

The Magna Carta is widely heralded to be the basis for many Constitution and charters in our day and throughout history. As can be seen, the Magan Carta itself – by the testimony of those who created it – goes back to the 11oo Charter under King Henry I.

A section of the Magna Carta that is now called clause 61 established a committee of 25 barons who could at any time meet and overrule the will of the King if he defied the provisions of the Charter. This became the building block for parliamentary government, backed by a written constitution. The Magna Carta forced the King to accept that his will was not arbitrary but subject to the "law of the land."

Clause 14 established taxation only through the representative council:

And for obtaining the common counsel of the kingdom [in regards to] the assessing of [a tax]...we will cause to be summoned the archbishops, bishops, abbots, earls, and greater barons, severally by our letters...

Clauses 39 and 40 express the due process rights of the accused:

No free man shall be arrested, or imprisoned, or deprived of his property, or outlawed, or exiled, or in any way destroyed, nor shall we go against him or send against him, unless by legal judgment of his peers, or by the law of the land.

To no one will we sell, to no one will we refuse or delay, right or justice.

Parliament and the Petition of Right of 1628

The next building block in our Constitution is the Petition of Rights and the strengthening of representative government in the form of Parliament. Although the Magna Carta laid the foundation for the development of Parliament, before the English Civil Wars the Parliament of England did not have a large permanent role in government. Parliament (as a result of the Magna Carta) was summoned by the monarch whenever the Crown required additional tax revenue. It was also subject to dissolution by the monarch at any time. Taxes were collected by the gentry and Parliaments allowed representatives of the gentry to meet, confer, and send policy-proposals to the monarch in the form of Bills. These representatives had no means of forcing their will upon the king—except by withholding the financial means required to execute his plans. **That sounds very much like 2011 as the House of Representatives attempts to defund the plans of a leader who takes on more of a kingly role with each passing day.**

In 1625 Charles I, son of King James I, ascended the throne. One of the first events to raise concerns over Charles's reign was his marriage to a French Roman Catholic princess. The people feared that the King's allegiances were not to his home country. They were concerned that he would favor some foreign power over England and that he would appoint ministers who also had questionable allegiances. Because of these concerns, Parliament refused to assign him the traditional right to collect taxes for his entire reign, deciding instead to grant it only on a provisional basis.

In 1627 Charles sent the unpopular Duke of Buckingham to help the French Huguenots. The relief expedition proved a fiasco and Parliament opened impeachment proceedings against the Duke. Charles responded by dissolving Parliament, reinforcing the impression that Charles wanted to avoid Parliamentary scrutiny of his ministers. Having dissolved Parliament and unable to raise money without it, the king assembled a new one in 1628. The new parliament forced the King to make concessions through the **Petition of Right** in order to obtain his taxes.

The **Petition of Right** of 1628 set forth specific protected liberties of the subjects. Among those liberties - that tax can be levied only by Parliament, that martial law may not be imposed in time of peace, and that prisoners must be able to challenge their detentions through the writ of *habeas corpus* and that troops may not be quartered against the will of residents.

Notice the reference to both the Magna Carta or Great Charter and previous laws:

...(T)hat whereas it is declared and enacted by a statute made in the time of the reign of King Edward I, commonly called **Stratutum de Tellagio non Concedendo**, that **no tallage** or aid **shall be laid or levied** by the king or his heirs in this realm, **without the good will and assent** of the archbishops, bishops, earls, barons, knights, burgesses, and other the freemen of the commonalty of this realm; and by authority of parliament holden in the five-and-twentieth year of the reign of King Edward III, it is declared and enacted, that from thenceforth **no person should be compelled to make any loans to the king against his will,** because such loans were against reason and the franchise of the land; and by other laws of this realm it is provided, that none should be charged by any charge or imposition called a benevolence, nor by such like charge; by which statutes before mentioned, and other the good laws and statutes of this realm, **your subjects have inherited this freedom,** that they should not be compelled to contribute to any tax, tallage, aid, or other like charge not set by common consent, in parliament.

Notice the assertion that the subjects had *"inherited"* these freedoms; they were asserting rights that they already possessed – just like our founding fathers.

Here are a few more extracts that show the foundation of our very own founding documents.

Against violations of due process:

"And whereas also by the statute called the **Great Charter of Liberties of England,** it is declared and enacted, that no freeman may be taken or imprisoned or be disseized of his freehold or liberties, or his free customs, or be outlawed or exiled, or in any manner destroyed, but by the lawful judgment of his peers, or by the law of the land."

Against quartering of soldiers:

"And whereas of late great companies of soldiers and mariners have been dispersed into divers counties of the realm, and the inhabitants against their wills have been compelled to receive them into their houses, and there to suffer them to sojourn against the laws and customs of this realm, and to the great grievance and vexation of the people."

Against Martial Law:

And whereas also by authority of parliament, in the five-and-twentieth year of the reign of King Edward III, it is declared and enacted, that no man shall be forejudged of life or limb against the form of **the Great Charter and the law of the land**; and by the said **Great Charter and other the laws and statutes of this your realm**, no man ought to be adjudged to death but by the laws established in this your realm, either by the customs of the same realm, or by acts of parliament: and whereas no offender of what kind soever is exempted from the proceedings to be used, and punishments to be inflicted by the laws and statutes of this your realm...

The Bishops Wars

The King avoided calling another Parliament for the next decade; and, during that time attempted to collect taxes in indirect and creative ways including a ship levy to support the Royal Navy. However, he caused the greatest opposition by instituting various religious dictates in the church, which included <u>Puritans being fined for not attending Anglican services</u>. In 1637 several <u>pamphleteers were arrested and had their ears cut off for protesting</u> these religious dictates. The King's authoritarian dealings with the Church would lead to the Bishops Wars of 1639 and 1640.

The King attempted to expand his church reforms throughout his realm and in 1637 he tried to dictate the program of worship and church structure in the Church of Scotland. Through the hierarchy of bishops which his father, King James I had introduced into the Church of Scotland in 1548, Charles forced upon them the Common Book of prayer. This sparked riots and lead to the National Covenant in Glasgow that asserted, among other things, that the church is to be led by a council of elders rather than powerful bishops.

King Charles decides to settle the issue by force. Charles in 1639 sent 20,000 soldiers to carry out his dictates. However, as neither of the main armies wanted to fight, the king was forced to sign the treaty Berwick, under which the king agreed that all disputed questions should be referred to another General Assembly or to the Parliament of Scotland. The new General Assembly then re-enacted all the measures passed by the Glasgow Assembly; and, the Scottish Parliament abolished the episcopacy and declared itself free from Royal control.

Charles I finally called an English parliament in April 1640 to pursue his endeavors against the Scots. Once convened, the parliament demanded redress of grievances, the abandonment of the royal claim to levy ship money, and a complete change in the ecclesiastical system. Charles dissolved parliament, launched a second campaign and was soundly defeated.

The King, near bankruptcy, had to summon another parliament to grant him the supplies which he needed to make payment to the triumphant Scots. The Parliament turned on the King, impeaching and executing his chief supporters. Charles went to Scotland in the autumn of 1641 and accepted all the decisions of the General Assembly of 1638 and of the Scottish Parliament of 1641, including confirming the **right of the Parliament to challenge the actions of his ministers** (or was that Czars?...)

English Civil Wars 1642-1651

This Parliament of 1640 was known as the **Long Parliament**. It believed Charles I to be moving to reestablish Catholicism in England, thereby subjecting England to the dictates of a foreign power, namely the Pope. Long Parliament was very hostile toward King Charles and used his defeats and the people's animosity as an opportunity to strengthen the power of Parliament. The legislators passed the **Triennial Act** which stated that a new Parliament should convene at least once every three years—without the King's summons, if necessary. Parliament also made it illegal for the king to impose taxes without Parliamentary consent, and later, gained control over the king's ministers. Most significantly, the **Parliament passed a law forbidding the King to dissolve it without its consent.**

The wars between the parliamentarians and royalist continued from 1642 to 1651 first between Charles I and the Long Parliament, then between Charles II and Rump Parliament. The wars ended in victory by the parliamentarians and left England, Scotland, and Ireland without a monarch. The parliament ruled until 1660 when Charles II was restored but only by consent of Parliament. **This strengthening of parliament would lead to the next block being laid in the development of our founding documents.**

The Glorious Revolution
and the English Bill of Rights of 1689

King James II ascended the throne in 1685 and picked up where Charles I left off. This sparked the Glorious Revolution, a final installment in the English civil wars. This revolution gave us the English Bill of Rights. That the monarch would rule by consent of the parliament was now codified and legally established in the English Bill of Rights of 1689.

The English Bill of Rights asserted the nation's *"ancient rights and liberties."* Among those liberties asserted was no taxation without consent of Parliament, right to petition King for redress of grievances, no quartering troops in peacetime, right to bear arms, freedom of speech, no excessive bail, no cruel and unusual punishments, right to trial by jury of peers, and right to due process.

England had officially been transformed into a parliamentary monarchy – **one more block in the foundation of American Liberty**.

Notice some of the grievances against King James. If you are familiar with the Declaration of Independence you will notice many similarities with the abuses of King George III. Bear in mind this is 100 years before the American Revolution. By the 1760s our founders realized that they had been down this road before. In fact Samuel Adams called for a gathering of the colonies *"as in the Glorious Revolution of 1689."*

Here are the issues in the Glorious Revolution:

Whereas the late King James the Second, by the assistance of divers evil counsellors, judges and ministers employed by him, did endeavour to subvert and extirpate the Protestant religion and the laws and liberties of this kingdom;

*By assuming and exercising a power of dispensing with and suspending of laws and **the execution of laws without consent of Parliament**; By committing and prosecuting divers worthy prelates for humbly petitioning to be excused from concurring to the said assumed power;*

By issuing and causing to be executed **a commission under the great seal** [agencies that answer only to the King] *for erecting a court called the Court of Commissioners for Ecclesiastical Causes;*

By **levying money** *for and to the use of the Crown by pretence of prerogative for other time and in* **other manner than the same was granted by Parliament;** [taxes outside of the authorized structure – creative/hidden taxes...perhaps James II would have loved to have had a carbon tax]

By raising and **keeping a standing army** *within this kingdom in time of peace without consent of Parliament, and* **quartering soldiers contrary to law;**

By causing several good subjects being Protestants **to be disarmed** *at the same time when papists were both armed and employed contrary to law;*

By violating the freedom of election of members to serve in Parliament;

By prosecutions in the Court of King's Bench for matters and causes cognizable only in Parliament, and by divers other arbitrary and illegal courses;

And whereas of late years partial corrupt and unqualified persons have been returned and served on juries in trials, and particularly divers jurors in trials for high treason which were not freeholders;

*And **excessive bail** hath been required of persons committed in criminal cases to elude the benefit of the laws made for the liberty of the subjects;*

*And **excessive fines** have been imposed;*

*And **illegal and cruel punishments** inflicted;*

*And several grants and promises made of **fines and forfeitures before any conviction or judgment** against the persons upon whom the same were to be levied;*

All which are utterly and directly contrary to the known laws and statutes and freedom of this realm;

In the following assertion of the citizens' rights, notice the similarities to our U.S. Bill of Rights. It should become clear to you that our founders did not invent the rights protected in our founding documents. The founders were simply reiterating the rights which they already possessed and securing greater protections for them. Keep in mind this is 100 years before the U.S. Bill of Rights:

That the pretended power of suspending the laws or the **execution of laws** *by regal authority* **without consent of Parliament** *is illegal;*

That the pretended power of dispensing with laws or the **execution of laws by regal authority,** *as it hath been assumed and exercised of late,* **is illegal;**

That the commission for erecting the late Court of Commissioners for Ecclesiastical Causes, and all other commissions and courts of like nature, are **illegal and pernicious;**

That **levying money** *for or to the use of the Crown by pretence of prerogative,* **without grant of Parliament,** *for longer time, or in other manner than the same is or shall be granted,* **is illegal;**

That it is the **right of the subjects to petition the king,** *and all commitments and prosecutions for such petitioning are illegal;*

*That the **raising or keeping a standing army** within the kingdom in **time of peace**, unless it be with consent of Parliament, **is against law;***

*That the **subjects** which are Protestants **may have arms for their defence** suitable to their conditions and as allowed by law;*

Notice the word above is "defence" NOT hunting or sport shooting.

That election of members of Parliament ought to be free;

*That the **freedom of speech and debates** or proceedings in Parliament ought **not to be impeached** or questioned in any court or place out of Parliament;*

*That **excessive bail** ought not to be required, nor excessive fines imposed, nor **cruel and unusual punishments** inflicted;*

*That **jurors** ought to be duly impanelled and returned, and jurors which pass upon men in trials for high treason ought to be **freeholders;***

*That all grants and promises of **fines and forfeitures** of particular persons **before conviction are illegal and void;***

*And that for **redress of all grievances**, and for the amending, strengthening and preserving of the laws, Parliaments ought to be held frequently.*

By the close of the Glorious revolution there were already thriving colonies in America (at least eight). Many colonists fled to the New World as a direct result of the English civil wars; but, by the 1760s tyranny was beginning to rise once more. The colonists recognized this tyranny because they were well acquainted with their history. A common refrain these days is that "we fell asleep." What that means is our ignorance of the history that brought us our American liberty allowed tyranny to sneak up on us. However, that was not the case for our founders.

"But what do we mean by the American Revolution? Do we mean the American war? The Revolution was effected before the war commenced. The Revolution was in the minds and hearts of the people." –John Adams

Tyranny Strikes Again

The first insidious weeds of tyranny were the writs of assistance enacted in 1760, a full decade and a half before the onset of civil war.

Writs of assistance were first authorized by an act of Parliament under Charles II and were issued by the Court of Exchequer to help customs officials search for smuggled goods. These writs were called "writs of assistance" because they enlisted sheriffs, other officials, and loyal subjects to "assist" the customs official in carrying out his duties.

The writs of assistance were general search warrants that did not expire, allowing customs officials to search anywhere for smuggled goods without having to obtain a specific warrant. In the colonies they began to be issued enabling British authorities to enter any colonist's home with no advance notice, no probable cause and no reason given. James Otis Jr. was an attorney who stood against these heinous acts. He provided *pro bono* representation to colonial merchants challenging the authority of the writs of assistance in 1761. He argued for nearly five hours in the Old Boston State House against these acts of tyranny.

Mr. Otis said these **writs of assistance** are

*"the **worst instrument[s] of arbitrary power**, the most destructive of English liberty and the fundamental principles of law, that ever w[ere] found in an English law book."* The writs of assistance *"place the liberty of every man in the hands of every petty officer."*

Today these writs of assistance are called National Security Letters (NSL's) and are authorized under the **Patriot Act**. The NSLs do not require a judge's warrant and can be performed with a handwritten letter from an FBI agent. By 2011 over 200,000 such searches had been performed without a judge's warrant and over 2 million searches of bank records (Suspicious Activities Report) had been conducted without a judge's warrant.

In July 2005, the FBI issued a National Security Letter to four Connecticut librarians. The letter sought computer subscriber data for a 45-minute period, during which a terrorist threat was *thought* to have been transmitted. In accordance with this letter, a gag order prevented the librarians from talking about the letter to anyone. The librarians refused to comply with the FBI's request and were arrested and federally prosecuted. Federal prosecutors eventually dropped the charges, but not until these librarians were indicted and brought before a federal judge under violations of the Patriot Act.

John Adams said of Otis' five-hour oration in the Boston State House against these abuses in his time:

"the child independence was then and there born, [for] every man of an immense crowded audience appeared to me to go away as I did, ready to take arms against writs of assistance."

In 2011 as our fourth and first amendments are being ravaged by both Republican and Democrat administrations - barely a peep...

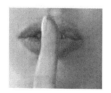

The oppressive actions by the royal government did not stop with the writs of assistance. In April 1764 Parliament passed the Sugar and Molasses Act. These laws were originally passed in 1733 at the insistence of the large plantation owners in the British West Indies (can you say lobbyists?)

The six-pence tax was never successfully collected, and so the Sugar Act actually cut the tax in half but stepped up enforcement. At the same time, the Sugar Act taxed the sugar, coffee, wine, and spices the colonists used, and also regulated the export of lumber and iron. This "excessive taxation and regulation" immediately impaired the colonial economy. In conjunction with the Sugar Act, parliament passed the Currency Act, which essentially assumed control of the colonial monetary system. The Currency Act also established "superior" Vice-admiralty courts to ensure rulings favorable to British interests.

In 1764 the colonies were in the midst of a depressed economy due to the protracted Seven Years' War, so these indirect taxes and restrictive laws were particularly grievous. In addition to the economic impact, the psychological impact was particularly offensive. The Sugar Act not only restricted the exports by the colonists, but gave an economic "leg up" to the British West Indies. This reinforced the second class status often attributed to the colonists by the British "mainlanders". The ports of New England were hit especially hard due to the taxes, regulation and government interference. **Many of the merchants were in danger of being driven out of the market into bankruptcy.**

The Birth of the "Tea Party" Movement

So in 1764 the first "grass roots" opposition to tyranny in the colonies took shape in the form of a **Committee of Correspondence** in Boston. The colonists did not have email, smart phones, Facebook or blogs, so the Committees of Correspondence served as a means of communication on issues that needed collective attention. The committee in Boston wrote to other colonies to rally united opposition to the Sugar Act and the Currency Act sparking anti-government protests among the colonists.

On the heels of these protests the Parliament, deciding to clamp down on the rebellious colonists, passed the first Stamp Act and Quartering Act of 1765 (10 years before the Revolution), and New York formed its Committee of Correspondence to rally resistance to the new taxes and tyranny. Massachusetts Bay committee then sent out letters urging other colonies to send representatives to a Stamp Act Congress in the fall.

As a decade of hostility between the royal government and the colonists rolled on, Boston set up the first Committee with the approval of a town meeting in 1772. By spring 1773, patriots decided to follow the Massachusetts system and began to set up their own Committees in each colony. By February 1774, 11 colonies had set up Committees of Correspondence. The Committees would eventually be the basis for the Continental Congress and the Continental Association of 1774. As the revolutionary period unfolded the Committees of Correspondence would become the basis for the future legislative bodies in America. <u>Yet it all began in 1764 as a citizen movement in response to an oppressive government that would not respond to or respect the wishes of the people.</u>

Two of the men behind the movement were Samuel Adams and the man we already met, James Otis Jr. John Adams said of attorney Otis:

"I have been young and now I am old, and I solemnly say I have never known a man whose love of country was more ardent or sincere, never one who suffered so much, never one whose service for any 10 years of his life were so important and essential to the cause of his country as those of Mr. Otis from 1760 to 1770."

Samuel Adams is well known for his role in the Boston Tea Party; but, the BTP was the culmination of his efforts beginning in 1764. A representative of the local Boston assembly and member of the Massachusetts House of Representatives, Samuel Adams had this to say in May 1764 in response to the heavy handed taxation and regulations of the crown:

"For if our Trade may be taxed, why not our Lands? Why not the Produce of our Lands & everything we possess or make use of? This we apprehend annihilates our Charter Right to govern & tax ourselves. It strikes at our British privileges, which as we have never forfeited them, we hold in common with our Fellow Subjects who are

Natives of Britain. If Taxes are laid upon us in any shape without our having a legal Representation where they are laid, are we not reduced from the Character of free Subjects to the miserable State of tributary Slaves?"[5]
Samuel Adams would later organize the Sons of Liberty which coordinated the famous Boston Tea Party of 1773.

There were also countless women involved in the struggle to reassert liberty of the colonists. One such heroine was **Penelope Barker,** whom we met in the introduction. Two others were **Abigail Adams** and her historian friend, **Mercy Otis Warren**. These were women of position with husbands of reputation, yet they shunned tea and spun their own flax and wool to boyott British textiles. Mercy's husband James Warren was the president of the Massachusetts Provincial Congress and member of the Sons of Liberty, but it was his wife, Mercy Otis Warren, whose patriotic efforts directly encouraged the war efforts. Mercy was a prolific writer of anti-British propaganda plays and a historian of the American Revolution. Her friend, Abigail Adams, said in 1773 that Mercy was "a sincere lover of [her] country." It was said that Mercy was so grieved by Great Britain's actions that she felt her nation to be "oppressed and insulted".

Hannah Winthrop wife of Dr. Winthrop, described Mercy as *"That noble patriotic spirit which sparkles must warm the heart that has the least sensibilities, especially must it invigorate a mind of a like fellow feeling for this once happy country. How often do we see people blind to their own interests precipitately maddening on to their own destruction!"*[6]

Mercy Otis Warren said of her nation:

"America stands armed with resolution and virtue; but she still recoils at the idea of drawing the sword against the nation from whence she derived her origin. Yet Britain, like an unnatural parent, is ready to plunge her dagger into the bosom of her affectionate offspring. But may we not yet hope for more lenient measures!"[7]

Much like the liberal media of today, the British attacked and portrayed these principled women as bad mothers and loose women. However, the colonists praised these ladies, and the women of the colonies followed their lead and began boycotting British goods.

As a result of the heroic effort of these and hundreds of other brave patriots, America took one step further in the founding of American liberty... from the consent of parliament - to the consent of the governed ...through the establishment of a representative form of government - our Constitutional Republic. Their work in crafting the documents from 1774-1789, that would be the foundation of our great Republic, was based on the wisdom and knowledge brought forward from the rich history of the colonists.

Conclusion

So, for over 700 years or more our founding fathers were developing the heritage of liberty that we enjoy today. They didn't just wake up one day and decide, hey let's think up a whole new concept of liberty - they just took the heritage that was already, deeply a part of who they were and brought it to its next logical stage - American Liberty. The foundation was already laid, they had already been through this; they didn't have to reinvent the wheel. In fact they made it better for people they didn't even know – us – the millions not yet born.

That is our heritage - not tearing down our American foundations, but making them better. We can only do that if we go back and reclaim the foundations that our nation is built upon. We don't need to reinvent the wheel, we just need to RECLAIM IT! We need to be reacquainted with that which has been ignored and hidden from us. We must reclaim our heritage of American Liberty by educating ourselves, our children and others of our deep history.

John Adams said:

Liberty must at all hazards be supported. We have a right to it, derived from our Maker. But if we had not, our fathers have earned and bought it for us, at the expense of their ease, their estates, their pleasure, and their blood. - <u>A Dissertation on the Canon and Feudal Law</u>, 1765

Notice John Adams said "our fathers," that is his fathers. These men looked to their "founding fathers" just as we do today. However, for some reason, we are not taught the history that helped our founding fathers give us this great nation. Could it be that some would have us to believe that our Republic is just a random experiment; rather than a refinement of ideals and lessons learned through centuries of experience? If we could be led to believe that America is just a 240-year-long experiment, then in times of difficulty, we could be convinced it has failed and that we must scrap it and replace it. You, dear reader, are no longer in the category of those who may be duped. You are awake; and, now you are armed!

We must heed the warnings of our founders and support liberty at all hazards. If we do not guard our liberty, then our republic will be weakened - either through intent or ignorance.

Make no mistake - the American ideal is still strong. America's founding principles are still valid. There is nothing wrong with the foundations of America. The problem is - we have strayed from these founding principles, and if we are to survive, then we must return to what makes America the most exceptional nation in human history. I firmly believe that America is a gift from God, and to whom much is given, much is required. May we be the heroes that our children need. May we be the guardians of the heart of America, and may God grant us a space of grace for "the millions not yet born!"

ATTENTION ATTENTION ATTENTION

Go back through this book, make notes, research what's in here. Learn it. Add more truth and teach it to your children, your family, your neighbors, your neighbors. Let's reclaim our history and rebuild America.

ATTENTION ATTENTION ATTENTION

Bibliography

1. Cohen, Charles (1981). "The 'Liberty or Death' Speech: A Note on Religion and Revolutionary Rhetoric". *The William and Mary Quarterly* **38** (4): 702–717

2. The Sharpened Quill The New Yorker, Accessed December 3, 2010,

3. Ketchum, Richard, *Divided Loyalties, How the American Revolution came to New York*, 2002,

4. Diane Silcox-Jarrett, "Penelope Barker, Leader of the Edenton Tea Party," in *Heroines of the American Revolution, America's Founding Mothers* (Chapel Hill, North Carolina: Green Angle Press, 1998), 17.

5. Fowler, William *Radical Puritan*, (Longman, 1997), 51-52

6. Ellet, Elizabeth F. The Women of the American Revolution, Third Edition, (New York: Baker and Scribner, 1849)

7. Ellet, Elizabeth F. The Women of the American Revolution, Third Edition, (New York: Baker and Scribner, 1849)

Please take some time to read the documents which make up the foundation of our Bill of Rights and Constitution.

1. A copy of the 1100 Charter of Liberties may be found online in the Internet Medieval Sourcebook.
   http://www.fordham.edu/halsall/source/hcoronation.html

2. A copy of the Magna Carta may be found online at the Constitution Society
   http://www.constitution.org/eng/magnacar.htm

3. A copy of the Petition of Right of 1628 may be found online at the Constitution Society
   http://www.constitution.org/eng/magnacar.htm

4. Another invaluable resource for Constitutional Interpretation are *Letters from the Federal Farmer*
   http://www.constitution.org/afp/fedfar00.htm

Other recommended Reading

The Federalist Papers
Common Sense by Thomas Payne
Founding Brothers by Joseph Ellis
1776 by David McCollough
John Adams by David McCollough
The Real George Washington by Jay Perry and Andrew Allison

Appendix A

English Bill of Rights of 1689

An Act Declaring the Rights and Liberties of the Subject and Settling the Succession of the Crown

Whereas the Lords Spiritual and Temporal and Commons assembled at Westminster, lawfully, fully and freely representing all the estates of the people of this realm, did upon the thirteenth day of February in the year of our Lord one thousand six hundred eighty-eight present unto their Majesties, then called and known by the names and style of William and Mary, prince and princess of Orange, being present in their proper persons, a certain declaration in writing made by the said Lords and Commons in the words following, viz.:

Whereas the late King James the Second, by the assistance of divers evil counsellors, judges and ministers employed by him, did endeavour to subvert and extirpate the Protestant religion and the laws and liberties of this kingdom;

By assuming and exercising a power of dispensing with and suspending of laws and the execution of laws without consent of Parliament;

By committing and prosecuting divers worthy prelates for humbly petitioning to be excused from concurring to the said assumed power;

By issuing and causing to be executed a commission under the great seal for erecting a court called the Court of Commissioners for Ecclesiastical Causes;

By levying money for and to the use of the Crown by pretence of prerogative for other time and in other manner than the same was granted by Parliament;

By raising and keeping a standing army within this kingdom in time of peace without consent of Parliament, and quartering soldiers contrary to law;

By causing several good subjects being Protestants to be disarmed at the same time when papists were both armed and employed contrary to law;

By violating the freedom of election of members to serve in Parliament;

By prosecutions in the Court of King's Bench for matters and causes cognizable only in Parliament, and by divers other arbitrary and illegal courses;

And whereas of late years partial corrupt and unqualified persons have been returned and served on juries in trials, and particularly divers jurors in trials for high treason which were not freeholders;

And excessive bail hath been required of persons committed in criminal cases to elude the benefit of the laws made for the liberty of the subjects;

And excessive fines have been imposed;

And illegal and cruel punishments inflicted;

And several grants and promises made of fines and forfeitures before any conviction or judgment against the persons upon whom the same were to be levied;

All which are utterly and directly contrary to the known laws and statutes and freedom of this realm;

And whereas the said late King James the Second having abdicated the government and the throne being thereby vacant, his Highness the prince of Orange (whom it hath pleased Almighty God to make the glorious instrument of delivering this kingdom from popery and arbitrary power) did (by the advice of the Lords Spiritual and Temporal and divers principal persons of the Commons) cause letters to be written to the Lords Spiritual and Temporal being Protestants, and other letters to the several counties, cities, universities, boroughs and cinque ports, for the choosing of such persons to represent them as were of right to be sent to Parliament, to meet and sit at Westminster upon the two and twentieth day of January in this year one thousand six hundred eighty and eight, in order to such an establishment as that their religion, laws and liberties might not again be in danger of being subverted, upon which letters elections having been accordingly made;

And thereupon the said Lords Spiritual and Temporal and Commons, pursuant to their respective letters and elections, being now assembled in a full and free representative of this nation, taking into their most serious consideration the best means for attaining the ends aforesaid, do in the first place (as their ancestors in like case have usually done) for the vindicating and asserting their ancient rights and liberties declare

That the pretended power of suspending the laws or the execution of laws by regal authority without consent of Parliament is illegal;

That the pretended power of dispensing with laws or the execution of laws by regal authority, as it hath been assumed and exercised of late, is illegal;

That the commission for erecting the late Court of Commissioners for Ecclesiastical Causes, and all other commissions and courts of like nature, are illegal and pernicious;

That levying money for or to the use of the Crown by pretence of prerogative, without grant of Parliament, for longer time, or in other manner than the same is or shall be granted, is illegal;

That it is the right of the subjects to petition the king, and all commitments and prosecutions for such petitioning are illegal;

That the raising or keeping a standing army within the kingdom in time of peace, unless it be with consent of Parliament, is against law;

That the subjects which are Protestants may have arms for their defence suitable to their conditions and as allowed by law;

That election of members of Parliament ought to be free;

That the freedom of speech and debates or proceedings in Parliament ought not to be impeached or questioned in any court or place out of Parliament;

That excessive bail ought not to be required, nor excessive fines imposed, nor cruel and unusual punishments inflicted;

That jurors ought to be duly impanelled and returned, and jurors which pass upon men in trials for high treason ought to be freeholders;

That all grants and promises of fines and forfeitures of particular persons before conviction are illegal and void;

And that for redress of all grievances, and for the amending, strengthening and preserving of the laws, Parliaments ought to be held frequently.

And they do claim, demand and insist upon all and singular the premises as their undoubted rights and liberties, and that no declarations, judgments, doings or proceedings to the prejudice of the people in any of the said premises ought in any wise to be drawn hereafter into consequence or example; to which demand of their rights they are particularly encouraged by the declaration of his Highness the prince of Orange as being the only means for obtaining a full redress and remedy therein. Having therefore an entire confidence that his said Highness the prince of Orange will perfect the deliverance so far advanced by him, and will still preserve them from the violation of their rights which they have here asserted, and from all other attempts upon their religion, rights and liberties, the said Lords Spiritual and Temporal and Commons assembled at Westminster do resolve that William and Mary, prince and princess of Orange, be and be declared king and queen of England, France and Ireland

and the dominions thereunto belonging, to hold the crown and royal dignity of the said kingdoms and dominions to them, the said prince and princess, during their lives and the life of the survivor to them, and that the sole and full exercise of the regal power be only in and executed by the said prince of Orange in the names of the said prince and princess during their joint lives, and after their deceases the said crown and royal dignity of the same kingdoms and dominions to be to the heirs of the body of the said princess, and for default of such issue to the Princess Anne of Denmark and the heirs of her body, and for default of such issue to the heirs of the body of the said prince of Orange. And the Lords Spiritual and Temporal and Commons do pray the said prince and princess to accept the same accordingly.

And that the oaths hereafter mentioned be taken by all persons of whom the oaths have allegiance and supremacy might be required by law, instead of them; and that the said oaths of allegiance and supremacy be abrogated.

I, A.B., do sincerely promise and swear that I will be faithful and bear true allegiance to their Majesties King William and Queen Mary. So help me God.

I, A.B., do swear that I do from my heart abhor, detest and abjure as impious and heretical this damnable doctrine and position, that princes excommunicated or deprived by the Pope or any authority of the see of Rome may be deposed or murdered by their subjects or any other whatsoever. And I do declare that no foreign prince, person, prelate, state or potentate hath or ought to have any jurisdiction, power, superiority, pre-eminence or authority, ecclesiastical or spiritual, within this realm. So help me God.

Upon which their said Majesties did accept the crown and royal dignity of the kingdoms of England, France and Ireland, and the dominions thereunto belonging, according to the resolution and desire of the said Lords and Commons contained in the said declaration. And thereupon their Majesties were pleased that the said Lords Spiritual and Temporal and Commons, being the two Houses of Parliament, should continue to sit, and with their Majesties' royal concurrence make effectual provision for the settlement of the religion, laws and liberties of this kingdom, so that the same for the future might not be in danger again of being subverted, to which the said Lords Spiritual and Temporal and Commons did agree, and proceed to act accordingly. Now in pursuance of the premises the said Lords Spiritual and Temporal and Commons in Parliament assembled, for the ratifying, confirming and establishing the said declaration and the articles, clauses, matters and things therein contained by the force of law made in due form by authority of Parliament, do pray that it may be declared and enacted that all and singular the rights and liberties asserted and claimed in the said declaration are the true, ancient and indubitable rights and liberties of the people of this kingdom, and so shall be esteemed, allowed, adjudged, deemed and taken to be; and that all and every the particulars aforesaid shall be firmly and strictly holden and observed as they are expressed in the said declaration, and all officers and ministers whatsoever shall serve their Majesties and their successors according to the same in all time to come. And the said Lords Spiritual and Temporal and Commons, seriously considering how it hath pleased Almighty God in his marvellous providence and merciful goodness to this nation to provide and preserve their said Majesties' royal persons most happily to reign over us upon the throne of their ancestors, for which they render unto him from the bottom of their hearts their humblest thanks and praises, do truly, firmly, assuredly and in the sincerity of their hearts think, and do hereby recognize, acknowledge and declare, that King James the Second having abdicated the government, and their Majesties having accepted the crown and royal dignity as aforesaid, their said Majesties did become, were, are and of right ought to be by the laws of this realm our sovereign liege lord and lady, king and queen of England, France and Ireland and the dominions thereunto belonging, in and to whose princely persons the royal state, crown and dignity of the said realms with all honours, styles, titles, regalities, prerogatives, powers, jurisdictions and authorities to the same belonging and appertaining are most fully, rightfully and entirely invested and incorporated, united and annexed. And for preventing all questions and divisions in this realm by reason of any pretended titles to the crown, and for preserving a certainty in the succession thereof, in and upon which the unity, peace, tranquility and safety of this nation doth under God wholly consist and depend, the said Lords Spiritual and Temporal and Commons do beseech their Majesties that it may be enacted, established and declared, that the crown and regal government of the said kingdoms and dominions, with all and singular the premises thereunto belonging and appertaining, shall be and continue to their said Majesties and the survivor of them during their lives and the life of the survivor of them, and that the entire, perfect and full exercise of the regal power and government be only in and executed by his Majesty in the names of both their Majesties during their joint lives; and after their deceases the said crown and premises shall be and remain to the heirs of the body of her Majesty, and for default of such issue to her Royal Highness the Princess Anne of Denmark and the heirs of the body of his said Majesty; and thereunto the said Lords Spiritual and Temporal and Commons do in the name of all the people aforesaid most humbly and faithfully submit themselves, their heirs and posterities for ever, and do faithfully promise that they will stand to, maintain and defend their said Majesties, and also the limitation and succession of the crown herein specified and contained, to the utmost of their powers with their lives and estates against all persons whatsoever that shall attempt anything to the contrary. And whereas it hath been found by experience that it is inconsistent with the safety and welfare of this Protestant kingdom to be governed by a popish prince, or by any king or queen marrying a papist, the said Lords Spiritual and Temporal and Commons do further pray that it may be enacted, that all and every person and persons that is, are or shall be reconciled to or shall hold communion with the see or Church of Rome, or shall profess the popish religion, or shall marry a papist, shall be excluded and be for ever incapable to inherit, possess or enjoy the crown and government of this realm and Ireland and the dominions thereunto belonging or any part of the same, or to have, use or exercise any regal power, authority or jurisdiction within the same; and in all and every such case or cases the people of these realms shall be and are hereby absolved of their allegiance; and the said crown and government shall from time to time descend to and be enjoyed by such person or persons being Protestants as should have inherited and enjoyed the same in case the said person or persons so reconciled, holding communion or professing or marrying as aforesaid were naturally dead; and that every king and queen of this realm who at any time hereafter shall come to and succeed in the imperial crown of this kingdom shall on the first day of the meeting of the first Parliament next after his or her coming to the crown, sitting in his or her throne in the

House of Peers in the presence of the Lords and Commons therein assembled, or at his or her coronation before such person or persons who shall administer the coronation oath to him or her at the time of his or her taking the said oath (which shall first happen), make, subscribe and audibly repeat the declaration mentioned in the statute made in the thirtieth year of the reign of King Charles the Second entitled, "An Act for the more effectual preserving the king's person and government by disabling papists from sitting in either House of Parliament." But if it shall happen that such king or queen upon his or her succession to the crown of this realm shall be under the age of twelve years, then every such king or queen shall make, subscribe and audibly repeat the same declaration at his or her coronation or the first day of the meeting of the first Parliament as aforesaid which shall first happen after such king or queen shall have attained the said age of twelve years. All which their Majesties are contented and pleased shall be declared, enacted and established by authority of this present Parliament, and shall stand, remain and be the law of this realm for ever; and the same are by their said Majesties, by and with the advice and consent of the Lords Spiritual and Temporal and Commons in Parliament assembled and by the authority of the same, declared, enacted and established accordingly.

II. And be it further declared and enacted by the authority aforesaid, that from and after this present session of Parliament no dispensation by "non obstante" of or to any statute or any part thereof shall be allowed, but that the same shall be held void and of no effect, except a dispensation be allowed of in such statute, and except in such cases as shall be specially provided for by one or more bill or bills to be passed during this present session of Parliament.

III. Provided that no charter or grant or pardon granted before the three and twentieth day of October in the year of our Lord one thousand six hundred eighty-nine shall be any ways impeached or invalidated by this Act, but that the same shall be and remain of the same force and

Appendix B

The US Bill of Rights

Amendment I

Congress shall make no law respecting an establishment of religion, or prohibiting the free exercise thereof; or abridging the freedom of speech, or of the press; or the right of the people peaceably to assemble, and to petition the Government for a redress of grievances.

Amendment II

A well regulated Militia, being necessary to the security of a free State, the right of the people to keep and bear Arms, shall not be infringed.

Amendment III

No Soldier shall, in time of peace be quartered in any house, without the consent of the Owner, nor in time of war, but in a manner to be prescribed by law.

Amendment IV

The right of the people to be secure in their persons, houses, papers, and effects, against unreasonable searches and seizures, shall not be violated, and no Warrants shall issue, but upon probable cause, supported by Oath or affirmation, and particularly describing the place to be searched, and the persons or things to be seized.

Amendment V

No person shall be held to answer for a capital, or otherwise infamous crime, unless on a presentment or indictment of a Grand Jury, except in cases arising in the land or naval forces, or in the Militia, when in actual service in time of War or public danger; nor shall any person be subject for the same offence to be twice put in jeopardy of life or limb; nor shall be compelled in any criminal case to be a witness against himself, nor be deprived of life, liberty, or property, without due process of law; nor shall private property be taken for public use, without just compensation.

Amendment VI

In all criminal prosecutions, the accused shall enjoy the right to a speedy and public trial, by an impartial jury of the State and district wherein the crime shall have been committed, which district shall have been previously ascertained by law, and to be informed of the nature and cause of the accusation; to be confronted with the witnesses against him; to have compulsory process for obtaining witnesses in his favor, and to have the Assistance of Counsel for his defence.

Amendment VII

In Suits at common law, where the value in controversy shall exceed twenty dollars, the right of trial by jury shall be preserved, and no fact tried by a jury, shall be otherwise re-examined in any Court of the United States, than according to the rules of the common law.

Amendment VIII

Excessive bail shall not be required, nor excessive fines imposed, nor cruel and unusual punishments inflicted.

Amendment IX

The enumeration in the Constitution, of certain rights, shall not be construed to deny or disparage others retained by the people.

Amendment X

The powers not delegated to the United States by the Constitution, nor prohibited by it to the States, are reserved to the States respectively, or to the people.

Appendix C

The Constitution of the United States

We the People of the United States, in Order to form a more perfect Union, establish Justice, insure domestic Tranquility, provide for the common defence, promote the general Welfare, and secure the Blessings of Liberty to ourselves and our Posterity, do ordain and establish this Constitution for the United States of America

Article I

Section 1. All legislative Powers herein granted shall be vested in a Congress of the United States, which shall consist of a Senate and House of Representatives.

Section 2. The House of Representatives shall be composed of Members chosen every second Year by the People of the several States, and the Electors in each State shall have the Qualifications requisite for Electors of the most numerous Branch of the State Legislature.

No Person shall be a Representative who shall not have attained to the age of twenty five Years, and been seven Years a Citizen of the United States, and who shall not, when elected, be an Inhabitant of that State in which he shall be chosen.

Representatives and direct Taxes shall be apportioned among the several States which may be included within this Union, according to their respective Numbers, which shall be determined by adding to the whole Number of free Persons, including those bound to Service for a Term of Years, and excluding Indians not taxed, three fifths of all other Persons. The actual Enumeration shall be made within three Years after the first Meeting of the Congress of the United States, and within every subsequent Term of ten Years, in such Manner as they shall by Law direct. The Number of Representatives shall not exceed one for every thirty Thousand, but each State shall have at Least one Representative; and until such enumeration shall be made, the State of New Hampshire shall be entitled to chuse three, Massachusetts eight, Rhode-Island and Providence Plantations one, Connecticut five, New-York six, New Jersey four, Pennsylvania eight, Delaware one, Maryland six, Virginia ten, North Carolina five, South Carolina five, and Georgia three.

When vacancies happen in the Representation from any State, the Executive Authority thereof shall issue Writs of Election to fill such Vacancies.

The House of Representatives shall chuse their Speaker and other Officers; and shall have the sole Power of Impeachment.

Section 3. The Senate of the United States shall be composed of two Senators from each State, chosen by the Legislature thereof, for six Years; and each Senator shall have one Vote.

Immediately after they shall be assembled in Consequence of the first Election, they shall be divided as equally as may be into three Classes. The Seats of the Senators of the first Class shall be vacated at the Expiration of the second Year, of the second Class at the Expiration of the fourth Year, and the third Class at the Expiration of the sixth Year, so that one third may be chosen every second Year; and if Vacancies happen by Resignation, or otherwise, during the Recess of the Legislature of any State, the Executive thereof may make temporary Appointments until the next Meeting of the Legislature, which shall then fill such Vacancies.

No Person shall be a Senator who shall not have attained to the Age of thirty Years, and been nine Years a Citizen of the United States and who shall not, when elected, be an Inhabitant of that State for which he shall be chosen.

The Vice President of the United States shall be President of the Senate, but shall have no Vote, unless they be equally divided.

The Senate shall chuse their other Officers, and also a President pro tempore, in the Absence of the Vice President, or when he shall exercise the Office of President of the United States.

The Senate shall have the sole Power to try all Impeachments. When sitting for that Purpose, they shall be on Oath or Affirmation. When the President of the United States is tried, the Chief Justice shall preside: And no Person shall be convicted without the Concurrence of two thirds of the Members present.

Judgment in Cases of Impeachment shall not extend further than to removal from Office, and disqualification to hold and enjoy any Office of Honor, Trust or Profit under the United States: but the Party convicted shall nevertheless be liable and subject to Indictment, Trial, Judgment and Punishment, according to Law.

Section 4. The Times, Places and Manner of holding Elections for Senators and Representatives, shall be prescribed in each State by the Legislature thereof; but the Congress may at any time by Law make or alter such Regulations, except as to the Places of chusing Senators.

The Congress shall assemble at least once in every Year, and such Meeting shall be on the first Monday in December, unless they shall by Law appoint a different Day.

Section 5. Each House shall be the Judge of the Elections, Returns and Qualifications of its own Members, and a Majority of each shall constitute a Quorum to do Business; but a smaller Number may adjourn from day to day, and may be authorized to compel the Attendance of absent Members, in such Manner, and under such Penalties as each House may provide.

Each House may determine the Rules of its Proceedings, punish its Members for disorderly Behaviour, and, with the Concurrence of two thirds, expel a Member.

Each House shall keep a Journal of its Proceedings, and from time to time publish the same, excepting such Parts as may in their Judgment require Secrecy; and the Yeas and Nays of the Members of either House on any question shall, at the Desire of one fifth of those Present, be entered on the Journal.

Neither House, during the Session of Congress, shall, without the Consent of the other, adjourn for more than three days, nor to any other Place than that in which the two Houses shall be sitting.

Section 6. The Senators and Representatives shall receive a Compensation for their Services, to be ascertained by Law, and paid out of the Treasury of the United States. They shall in all Cases, except Treason, Felony and Breach of the Peace, be privileged from Arrest during their Attendance at the Session of their respective Houses, and in going to and returning from the same; and for any Speech or Debate in either House, they shall not be questioned in any other Place.

No Senator or Representative shall, during the Time for which he was elected, be appointed to any civil Office under the Authority of the United States, which shall have been created, or the Emoluments whereof shall have been encreased during such time: and no Person holding any Office under the United States, shall be a Member of either House during his Continuance in Office.

Section 7. All Bills for raising Revenue shall originate in the House of Representatives; but the Senate may propose or concur with Amendments as on other Bills.

Every Bill which shall have passed the House of Representatives and the Senate, shall, before it become a Law, be presented to the President of the United States; if he approve he shall sign it, but if not he shall return it, with his Objections to that House in which it shall have originated, who shall enter the Objections at large on their Journal, and proceed to reconsider it. If after such Reconsideration two thirds of that House shall agree to pass the Bill, it shall be sent, together with the Objections, to the other House, by which it shall likewise be reconsidered, and if approved by two thirds of that House, it shall become a Law. But in all such Cases the Votes of both Houses shall be determined by Yeas and Nays, and the Names of the Persons voting for and against the Bill shall be entered on the Journal of each House respectively. If any Bill shall not be returned by the President within ten Days (Sundays excepted) after it shall have been presented to him, the Same shall be a Law, in like Manner as if he had signed it, unless the Congress by their Adjournment prevent its Return, in which Case it shall not be a Law.

Every Order, Resolution, or Vote to which the Concurrence of the Senate and House of Representatives may be necessary (except on a question of Adjournment) shall be presented to the President of the United States; and before the Same shall take Effect, shall be approved by him, or being disapproved by him, shall be repassed by two thirds of the Senate and House of Representatives, according to the Rules and Limitations prescribed in the Case of a Bill.

Section 8. The Congress shall have Power To lay and collect Taxes, Duties, Imposts and Excises, to pay the Debts and provide for the common Defence and general Welfare of the United States; but all Duties, Imposts and Excises shall be uniform throughout the United States;

To borrow Money on the credit of the United States;

To regulate Commerce with foreign Nations, and among the several States, and with the Indian Tribes;

To establish an uniform Rule of Naturalization, and uniform Laws on the subject of Bankruptcies throughout the United States;

To coin Money, regulate the Value thereof, and of foreign Coin, and fix the Standard of Weights and Measures;

To provide for the Punishment of counterfeiting the Securities and current Coin of the United States;

To establish Post Offices and post Roads;

To promote the Progress of Science and useful Arts, by securing for limited Times to Authors and Inventors the exclusive Right to their respective Writings and Discoveries;

To constitute Tribunals inferior to the supreme Court;

To define and punish Piracies and Felonies committed on the high Seas, and Offences against the Law of Nations;

To declare War, grant Letters of Marque and Reprisal, and make Rules concerning Captures on Land and Water;

To raise and support Armies, but no Appropriation of Money to that Use shall be for a longer Term than two Years;

To provide and maintain a Navy;

To make Rules for the Government and Regulation of the land and naval Forces;

To provide for calling forth the Militia to execute the Laws of the Union, suppress Insurrections and repel Invasions;

To provide for organizing, arming, and disciplining, the Militia, and for governing such Part of them as may be employed in the Service of the United States, reserving to the States respectively, the Appointment of the Officers, and the Authority of training the Militia according to the discipline prescribed by Congress;

To exercise exclusive Legislation in all Cases whatsoever, over such District (not exceeding ten Miles square) as may, by Cession of particular States, and the Acceptance of Congress, become the Seat of the Government of the United States, and to exercise like Authority over all Places purchased by the Consent of the Legislature of the State in which the Same shall be, for the Erection of Forts, Magazines, Arsenals, dock-Yards, and other needful Buildings;--And

To make all Laws which shall be necessary and proper for carrying into Execution the foregoing Powers, and all other Powers vested by this Constitution in the Government of the United States, or in any Department or Officer thereof.

Section 9. The Migration or Importation of such Persons as any of the States now existing shall think proper to admit, shall not be prohibited by the Congress prior to the Year one thousand eight hundred and eight, but a Tax or duty may be imposed on such Importation, not exceeding ten dollars for each Person.

The Privilege of the Writ of Habeas Corpus shall not be suspended, unless when in Cases of Rebellion or Invasion the public Safety may require it.

No Bill of Attainder or ex post facto Law shall be passed.

No Capitation, or other direct, Tax shall be laid, unless in Proportion to the Census or Enumeration herein before directed to be taken.

No Tax or Duty shall be laid on Articles exported from any State.

No Preference shall be given by any Regulation of Commerce or Revenue to the Ports of one State over those of another: nor shall Vessels bound to, or from, one State, be obliged to enter, clear or pay Duties in another.

No Money shall be drawn from the Treasury, but in Consequence of Appropriations made by Law; and a regular Statement and Account of Receipts and Expenditures of all public Money shall be published from time to time.

No Title of Nobility shall be granted by the United States: And no Person holding any Office of Profit or Trust under them, shall, without the Consent of the Congress, accept of any present, Emolument, Office, or Title, of any kind whatever, from any King, Prince, or foreign State.

Section 10. No State shall enter into any Treaty, Alliance, or Confederation; grant Letters of Marque and Reprisal; coin Money; emit Bills of Credit; make any Thing but gold and silver Coin a Tender in Payment of Debts; pass any Bill of Attainder, ex post facto Law, or Law impairing the Obligation of Contracts, or grant any Title of Nobility.

No State shall, without the Consent of the Congress, lay any Imposts or Duties on Imports or Exports, except what may be absolutely necessary for executing it's inspection Laws: and the net Produce of all Duties and Imposts, laid by any State on Imports or Exports, shall be for the Use of the Treasury of the United States; and all such Laws shall be subject to the Revision and Controul of the Congress.

No State shall, without the Consent of Congress, lay any Duty of Tonnage, keep Troops, or Ships of War in time of Peace, enter into any Agreement or Compact with another State, or with a foreign Power, or engage in War, unless actually invaded, or in such imminent Danger as will not admit of delay.

Article II

Section 1. The executive Power shall be vested in a President of the United States of America. He shall hold his Office during the Term of four Years, and, together with the Vice President, chosen for the same Term, be elected, as follows:

Each State shall appoint, in such Manner as the Legislature thereof may direct, a Number of Electors, equal to the whole Number of Senators and Representatives to which the State may be entitled in the Congress: but no Senator or Representative, or Person holding an Office of Trust or Profit under the United States, shall be appointed an Elector.

The Electors shall meet in their respective States, and vote by Ballot for two Persons, of whom one at least shall not be an Inhabitant of the same State with themselves. And they shall make a List of all the Persons voted for, and of the Number of Votes for each; which List they shall sign and certify, and transmit sealed to the Seat of the Government of the United States, directed to the President of the Senate. The President of the Senate shall, in the

Presence of the Senate and House of Representatives, open all the Certificates, and the Votes shall then be counted. The Person having the greatest Number of Votes shall be the President, if such Number be a Majority of the whole Number of Electors appointed; and if there be more than one who have such Majority, and have an equal Number of Votes, then the House of Representatives shall immediately chuse by Ballot one of them for President; and if no Person have a Majority, then from the five highest on the List the said House shall in like Manner chuse the President. But in chusing the President, the Votes shall be taken by States, the Representation from each State having one Vote; A quorum for this Purpose shall consist of a Member or Members from two thirds of the States, and a Majority of all the States shall be necessary to a Choice. In every Case, after the Choice of the President, the Person having the greatest Number of Votes of the Electors shall be the Vice President. But if there should remain two or more who have equal Votes, the Senate shall chuse from them by Ballot the Vice President.

The Congress may determine the Time of chusing the Electors, and the Day on which they shall give their

Votes; which Day shall be the same throughout the United States.

No Person except a natural born Citizen, or a Citizen of the United States, at the time of the Adoption of this Constitution, shall be eligible to the Office of President; neither shall any Person be eligible to that Office who shall not have attained to the Age of thirty five Years, and been fourteen Years a Resident within the United States.

In Case of the Removal of the President from Office, or of his Death, Resignation, or Inability to discharge the Powers and Duties of the said Office, the Same shall devolve on the Vice President, and the Congress may by Law provide for the Case of Removal, Death, Resignation or Inability, both of the President and Vice President, declaring what Officer shall then act as President, and such Officer shall act accordingly, until the Disability be removed, or a President shall be elected.

The President shall, at stated Times, receive for his Services, a Compensation, which shall neither be encreased nor diminished during the Period for which he shall have been elected, and he shall not receive within that Period any other Emolument from the United States, or any of them.

Before he enter on the Execution of his Office, he shall take the following Oath or Affirmation:--"I do solemnly swear (or affirm) that I will faithfully execute the Office of President of the United States, and will to the best of my Ability, preserve, protect and defend the Constitution of the United States."

Section 2. The President shall be Commander in Chief of the Army and Navy of the United States, and of the Militia of the several States, when called into the actual Service of the United States; he may require the Opinion, in writing, of the principal Officer in each of the executive Departments, upon any Subject relating to the Duties of their respective Offices, and he shall have Power to grant Reprieves and Pardons for Offences against the United States, except in Cases of Impeachment.

He shall have Power, by and with the Advice and Consent of the Senate, to make Treaties, provided two thirds of the Senators present concur; and he shall nominate, and by and with the Advice and Consent of the Senate, shall appoint Ambassadors, other public Ministers and Consuls,

Judges of the supreme Court, and all other Officers of the United States, whose Appointments are not herein otherwise provided for, and which shall be established by Law: but the Congress may by Law vest the Appointment of such inferior Officers, as they think proper, in the President alone, in the Courts of Law, or in the Heads of Departments.

The President shall have Power to fill up all Vacancies that may happen during the Recess of the Senate, by granting Commissions which shall expire at the End of their next Session.

Section 3. He shall from time to time give to the Congress Information of the State of the Union, and recommend to their Consideration such Measures as he shall judge necessary and expedient; he may, on extraordinary Occasions, convene both Houses, or either of them, and in Case of Disagreement between them, with Respect to the Time of Adjournment, he may adjourn them to such Time as he shall think proper; he shall receive Ambassadors and other public Ministers; he shall take Care that the Laws be faithfully executed, and shall Commission all the Officers of the United States.

Section 4. The President, Vice President and all civil Officers of the United States, shall be removed from Office on Impeachment for, and Conviction of, Treason, Bribery, or other high Crimes and Misdemeanors.

Article III

Section 1. The judicial Power of the United States, shall be vested in one supreme Court, and in such inferior Courts as the Congress may from time to time ordain and establish. The Judges, both of the supreme and inferior Courts, shall hold their Offices during good Behaviour, and shall, at stated Times, receive for their Services, a Compensation, which shall not be diminished during their Continuance in Office.

Section 2. The judicial Power shall extend to all Cases, in Law and Equity, arising under this Constitution, the Laws of the United States, and Treaties made, or which shall be made, under their Authority;--to all Cases affecting Ambassadors, other public Ministers and Consuls;--to all Cases of admiralty and maritime Jurisdiction;--to Controversies to which the United States shall be a Party;--to Controversies between two or more States;--between a State and Citizens of another State;--between Citizens of different States;--between Citizens of the same State claiming Lands under Grants of different States, and between a State, or the Citizens thereof, and foreign States, Citizens or Subjects.

In all Cases affecting Ambassadors, other public Ministers and Consuls, and those in which a State shall be Party, the supreme Court shall have original Jurisdiction. In all the other Cases before mentioned, the supreme Court shall have appellate Jurisdiction, both as to Law and Fact, with such Exceptions, and under such Regulations as the Congress shall make.

The Trial of all Crimes, except in Cases of Impeachment, shall be by Jury; and such Trial shall be held in the State where the said Crimes shall have been committed; but when not committed within any State, the Trial shall be at such Place or Places as the Congress may by Law have directed.

Section 3. Treason against the United States, shall consist only in levying War against them, or in adhering to their Enemies, giving them Aid and Comfort. No Person shall be convicted of Treason unless on the Testimony of two Witnesses to the same overt Act, or on Confession in open Court.

The Congress shall have Power to declare the Punishment of Treason, but no Attainder of Treason shall work Corruption of Blood, or Forfeiture except during the Life of the Person attainted.

Article IV

Section 1. Full Faith and Credit shall be given in each State to the public Acts, Records, and judicial Proceedings of every other State. And the Congress may by general Laws prescribe the Manner in which such Acts, Records, and Proceedings shall be proved, and the Effect thereof.

Section 2. The Citizens of each State shall be entitled to all Privileges and Immunities of Citizens in the several States.

A Person charged in any State with Treason, Felony, or other Crime, who shall flee from Justice, and be found in another State, shall on Demand of the executive Authority of the State from which he fled, be delivered up, to be removed to the State having Jurisdiction of the Crime.

No Person held to Service or Labour in one State, under the Laws thereof, escaping into another, shall, in

Consequence of any Law or Regulation therein, be discharged from such Service or Labour, but shall be delivered up on Claim of the Party to whom such Service or Labour may be due.

Section 3. New States may be admitted by the Congress into this Union; but no new States shall be formed or erected within the Jurisdiction of any other State; nor any State be formed by the Junction of two or more States, or Parts of States, without the Consent of the Legislatures of the States concerned as well as of the Congress.

The Congress shall have Power to dispose of and make all needful Rules and Regulations respecting the Territory or other Property belonging to the United States; and nothing in this Constitution shall be so construed as to Prejudice any Claims of the United States, or of any particular State.

Section 4. The United States shall guarantee to every State in this Union a Republican Form of Government, and shall protect each of them against Invasion; and on Application of the Legislature, or of the Executive (when the Legislature cannot be convened) against domestic Violence.

Article V

The Congress, whenever two thirds of both Houses shall deem it necessary, shall propose Amendments to this Constitution, or, on the Application of the Legislatures of two thirds of the several States, shall call a Convention for proposing Amendments, which, in either Case, shall be valid to all Intents and Purposes, as Part of this Constitution, when ratified by the Legislatures of three fourths of the several States, or by Conventions in three fourths thereof, as the one or the other Mode of Ratification may be proposed by the Congress; Provided that no Amendment which may be made prior to the Year One thousand eight hundred and eight shall in any Manner affect the first and fourth Clauses in the Ninth Section of the first Article; and that no State, without its Consent, shall be deprived of its equal Suffrage in the Senate.

Article VI

All Debts contracted and Engagements entered into, before the Adoption of this Constitution, shall be as valid against the United States under this Constitution, as under the Confederation.

This Constitution, and the Laws of the United States which shall be made in Pursuance thereof; and all Treaties made, or which shall be made, under the Authority of the United States, shall be the supreme Law of the Land; and the Judges in every State shall be bound thereby, any Thing in the Constitution or Laws of any State to the Contrary notwithstanding.

The Senators and Representatives before mentioned, and the Members of the several State Legislatures, and all executive and judicial Officers, both of the United States and of the several States, shall be bound by Oath or Affirmation, to support this Constitution; but no religious Test shall ever be required as a Qualification to any Office or public Trust under the United States.

Article VII

The Ratification of the Conventions of nine States, shall be sufficient for the Establishment of this Constitution between the States so ratifying the Same.

Done in Convention by the Unanimous Consent of the States present the Seventeenth Day of September in the Year of our Lord one thousand seven hundred and Eighty seven and of the Independence of the United States of America the Twelfth

Appendix D

Articles by KrisAnne

Several of these articles can be found at www.krisannehall.com and www.boogai.net. They may be copied and freely distributed with proper credit to the author.

Historic TEA party Roots
247 years of Resisting Tyranny

by KrisAnne Hall

I recently read with joy a conservative blogger's attempt to connect the TEA party movement to its historic roots; a topic I have been meaning to write about for months now. The blogger rightly said that the "the historical precedent for the TPM wasn't the Tea Party event in Boston Harbor on December 16, 1773." I actually uttered an "Amen, brother!" He went on to describe the Continental Association established on October 20, 1774 by the First Continental Congress in response to the Intolerable Acts. That's when I realized that I have waited long enough to write this article.

The fact is the Continental Association of 1774 (10 months after the Boston Tea Party) is about 10 years too late. The first organized opposition to a tyrannical government in the colonies came in 1764 in the form of the Committees of Correspondence.

In April 1764 Parliament passed the Sugar and Molasses Act. These laws were originally passed in 1733 at the insistence of the large plantation owners in the British West Indies (can you say lobbyists?) The six-pence tax was never successfully collected, and so the Sugar Act actually cut the tax in half but stepped up enforcement. At the same time, the Sugar Act taxed the sugar, coffee, wine, and spices the colonists used, and also regulated the export of lumber and iron. This "excessive taxation and regulation" immediately impaired the colonial economy. In conjunction with the Sugar Act, parliament passed the Currency Act, which essentially assumed control of the colonial monetary system. The Currency Act also established "superior" Vice-admiralty courts to ensure rulings favorable to British interests.

In 1764 the colonies were in the midst of a depressed economy due to the protracted Seven Years' War, so these indirect taxes and restrictive laws were particularly grievous. In addition to the economic impact, the psychological impact was particularly offensive. The Sugar Act not only restricted the exports by the colonists, but gave an economic "leg up" to the British West Indies. This reinforced the second class status often attributed to the colonists by the British "mainlanders". The ports of New England were hit especially hard due to the taxes, regulation and government interference. Many of the merchants were in danger of being driven out of the market into bankruptcy.

So in 1764 the first "grass roots" opposition to tyranny in the colonies took shape in the form of a Committee of Correspondence in Boston. The colonists did not have email, smart phones, Facebook or blogs, so the Committees of Correspondence served as a means of communication on issues that needed collective attention. The committee in Boston wrote to other colonies to rally united opposition to the Sugar Act and the Currency Act sparking anti-government protests among the colonists.

On the heels of these protests the Parliament, deciding to clamp down on the rebellious colonists, passed the first Stamp Act and Quartering Act of 1765, and New York formed its Committee of Correspondence to rally resistance to the new taxes and tyranny. Massachusetts Bay committee then sent out letters urging other colonies to send representatives to a Stamp Act Congress in the fall.

As a decade of hostility between the royal government and the colonists rolled on, Boston set up the first Committee with the approval of a town meeting 1772. By spring 1773, patriots decided to follow the Massachusetts system and began to set up their own Committees in each colony. By February 1774, 11 colonies had set up Committees of Correspondence. The Committees would eventually be the basis for the Continental Congress and the Continental Association of 1774. As the revolutionary period unfolded the Committees of Correspondence would become the basis for the future legislative bodies in America. Yet it all began in 1764 as a citizen movement in response to an oppressive government that would not respond to or respect the wishes of the people.

Two of the men behind the movement were Samuel Adams and James Otis Jr.

Mr. Otis was an attorney who had gained notoriety for his *pro bono* representation of colonial merchants challenging the authority of the writs of assistance in 1761. These writs enabled British authorities to enter any colonist's home with no advance notice, no probable cause and no reason given. (Today these writs are called national security letters and are authorized under the Patriot Act.) John Adams said of Otis' five-hour oration in the Boston State House that:

"the child independence was then and there born, [for] every man of an immense crowded audience appeared to me to go away as I did, ready to take arms against writs of assistance."

Also speaking of Otis, John Adams said,

"I have been young and now I am old, and I solemnly say I have never known a man whose love of country was more ardent or sincere, never one who suffered so much, never one whose service for any 10 years of his life were so important and essential to the cause of his country as those of Mr. Otis from 1760 to 1770."

Better known was Samuel Adams, a representative of the local Boston assembly and member of the Massachusetts House of Representatives. Samuel Adams had this to say in May 1764:

"For if our Trade may be taxed, why not our Lands? Why not the Produce of our Lands & everything we possess or make use of? This we apprehend annihilates our Charter Right to govern & tax ourselves. It strikes at our British privileges, which as we have never forfeited them, we hold in common with our Fellow Subjects who are Natives of Britain. If Taxes are laid upon us in any shape without our having a legal Representation where they are laid, are we not reduced from the Character of free Subjects to the miserable State of tributary Slaves?"

Samuel Adams would later organize the Sons of Liberty which coordinated the famous Boston Tea Party of 1773.

But let's not forget the ladies of the TEA party movement. Penelope Barker of Edenton, North Carolina organized the Edenton Tea Party in 1774. In the home of her friend Elizabeth King, she and 50 other women signed a declaration and sent it to be published in a London newspaper. In part the declaration said:

"Maybe it has only been men who have protested the king up to now. That only means we women have taken too long to let our voices be heard. We are signing our names to a document, not hiding ourselves behind costumes like the men in Boston did at their tea party. The British will know who we are...We, the aforesaid Ladys will not promote ye wear of any manufacturer from England until such time that all acts which tend to enslave our Native country shall be repealed."

Much like the liberal media of today these principled women were attacked and portrayed by the British as bad mothers and loose women. However, the colonists praised these ladies and the women of the colonies followed their lead and began boycotting British goods.

In light of historical fact, it is clear to any rational and reasonable mind that the modern TEA party movement is not a modern movement at all. The TEA party represents the heart of the American ideal of liberty and self-government. These brave men and women did not sit idly by in the face of oppression and tyranny because they understood their history and knew their rights. They understood that their rights came from God and had been guaranteed to them beginning at the 1100 Charter of Liberties, through the Magna Carta of 1215, and the English Bill of Rights of 1688. Their liberty was not a modern development and neither is ours. That is why, in spite of Rachel Maddow's pronouncement that the TEA party is over because of small rallies, the TEA party is not going away. It has been here for 247 years and will continue as long as the founding principles of America still burn in the hearts of patriots.

Faisal Shahzad and the 800lb Gorilla

By KrisAnne Hall

In the infamous words of Rahm Emanauel, "You never want a serious crisis to go to waste." And we have had plenty recently. It seems as if a crisis today is like the weather in St. Louis, if you don't like it just wait five minutes and it will change. The problem is, as each crisis changes, so does the attention of the people. It becomes a huge shell game where the people's attention is diverted from one crisis to the next, all the while the powers that be remember to never let a serious crisis go to waste.

Thomas Jefferson said, "the price of freedom is eternal vigilance." According to Jefferson, we should be distracted, we should be vigilant against every enemy of freedom. That precept brings me to Faisal Shahzad and the crisis of his Constitutional rights. For those that may have forgotten Mr. Shahzad in the flurry of new crises, Mr. Shahzad was the prime suspect in the May 1, 2010, Times Square car bomb attempt, to which he has reportedly confessed. Around this crisis flurried the question of whether Mr. Shahzad should be entitled to his Miranda rights. I'm sure many have heard about Miranda rights, as cop shows are extremely popular today.

However, how many actually understand the origin of these rights and why we have them?

Miranda v. Arizona (1966) was a landmark case involving confessions. Ernesto Miranda had signed a statement confessing the crime, but the Supreme Court held that the confession was inadmissible because the defendant had not been warned of his rights. What rights were those exactly? They were the rights espoused to every citizen of the United States via the 5th and 6th Amendments of the Constitution. The section of the 5th Amendment that is applicable to the Miranda case is as follows:

No person shall be held to answer for a capital, or otherwise infamous crime, nor shall be compelled in any criminal case to be a witness against himself,

The **Self-Incrimination Clause** is based on the idea that people cannot be forced to testify against themselves against their will, an idea that came to America from the English common law. This idea did not become established law in England until the 1700s. Prior to this time, people could be forced to testify against themselves, and this evidence was admissible in court, even if the evidence was obtained by torturing the witness.

These tactics had been used primarily to extinguish any political or religious belief that differed from the Royal government's. Forcing "confessions" by torture was common to many European nations. In England the notorious Star Chamber was the court in which many religious dissenters were tried and executed for their beliefs. A religious dissenter means one who "dissented" from the state sanctioned Church of England.

It wasn't until 1638, that the idea that it is a "natural right" that people should not be forced to testify against themselves came to be popularly accepted. At the time, all published literature had to be approved by the government. Since the Puritan literature disagreed with the government's official church, the literature was banned. The English Puritans embraced that the idea that the government should not force people to testify against themselves or be tortured. Since most of the early colonists in America were Puritans, who had left England because of the religious persecution, they carried this idea with them to the New World.

By the time the Revolutionary War ended, the belief was so widely held that six states wrote in anti-**self-incrimination clauses** into their constitutions. Several states recommended also recommended an anti-**self-incrimination clause** be added to the Constitution.

The second half of the Miranda warning incorporates the following portion of the 6th Amendment:

"In all criminal prosecutions, the accused shall enjoy the right to have the Assistance of Counsel for his defense."

The roots of all American laws are found in English law. In England, people who were charged with felonies had no right to hire a private attorney, though it was allowed sometimes in special circumstances. After the Glorious Revolution in 1688, Parliament passed a law allowing people accused of treason the right to be represented by an attorney at trial, but this right did not extend to any other classes of crime. All the way up until 1836, with the passage of the Prisoners' Counsel Act, this right was denied to people charged with nearly all serious crimes in England.

The early American colonies generally brought English law with them, so most colonies also barred serious criminal defendants from obtaining a lawyer. This practice varied from colony to colony with some colonies appointing lawyers in some circumstances. Sometimes people were represented by an outside attorney, but it was done so freely by attorneys as an act of good will, for trial experience and for personal publicity. In some cases, these attorneys were paid at the public's expense.

By the time of the Revolutionary War, most of the educated class believed that a person should have the right to hire an outside attorney or to even represent himself at trial, if he chose to do so and had the financial means to do so. Representing oneself at trial was very common in these days. Hiring an outside attorney to represent oneself was more rare and did not come into prevalence until the first half of the 1800's.

Attorney General **Eric** Holder wants to make the requirement for Miranda more "flexible". Although he did not elaborate, he did say he would seek to make the exception "consistent with the public safety concerns that we now have in the 21st century as opposed to the public safety concerns that we had back in the 1980s."

What Mr. Holder is referring to is the pivotal Supreme
Court case, *New York v. Quarles* (1984) that carved out a
'public safety exception'. In *New York v. Quarles*, 467
U.S. 649 (1984), the Court held that in limited
circumstances where legitimate concerns about public
safety exist, evidence and statements are admissible in a
trial even when a suspect is not informed of his Miranda
rights. Although the circumstances that define 'public
safety' were established by New York v. Quarles, it
appears that Mr. Holder believes that Congress should
now broaden those standards.

**The question that Mr. Holder wants to distract with is,
should Mr. Shahzad be afforded the same
Constitutional rights as every other citizen of the
United States? Without out great thought or
speculation the answer to that question should be a
most emphatic YES! Every *citizen* should be afforded
every Constitutional protection that our founding
fathers fought for and our brave military have bled
and died for. It should not be up to the government to
determine when and how the Constitution applies to
its citizens. We must remember the reasons we have
these rights. Patrick Henry told us that "The
Constitution is not an instrument for the government**

to restrain the people, it is an instrument for the people to restrain the government," and George Washington furthered that thought by saying, "Government is not reason; it is not eloquence. It is force. And force, like fire, is a dangerous servant and a fearful master." We cannot allow the government to have that type of power. And we don't have to when we open our eyes to the 800lb gorilla standing in the room.

Mr. Shahzad was a citizen of the United States. That is the issue that we should be addressing. We need to look at the circumstances under which Mr. Shahzad became a citizen of this country and then question how that was allowed to happen.

Mr. Shahzad was born in Pakistan. In December 1998 he was granted an F-1 student visa. In 1999 he was placed on a US Customs (later merged into DHS) travel lookout list called the "Traveler Enforcement Compliance System. Between 1999 and 2008 Mr. Shahzad brought approximately $80,000 cash or cash instruments into the United States.

In spite of being on this watch list, he was granted U.S. citizenship on April 17, 2009, due to his marriage to his wife. A few weeks later, he abruptly quit his job and stopped making payments on his house, defaulting on the $218,400 mortgage. After an 8 month stint in Pakistan, Shahzad came back to the U.S. in February 2010. There is no record he had any job since returning. Yet he drove an Isuzu and paid $1,150 per month to rent an apartment in Bridgeport, CT, never missing a payment. He clearly had plenty of cash. Shahzad slapped down $1,300 in $100 dollar bills to pay for the used SUV that was found smoking, rigged with explosives, in Times Square last Saturday.

A CBS News analysis estimates he spent at least $2,000 to make the bomb. He reportedly had at least one gun estimated to be worth $400. On Monday night when he tried to flee, he forked over an estimated $800 in cash to pay for a one-way ticket to Islamabad, Pakistan via Dubai, UAE.

The REAL question is not should a citizen of the United States be afforded Constitutional protection. The real question is, why Shahzad was every granted citizenship. Our failing is not in the Constitution, it is in the immigration process. Why then isn't Mr. Holder trying to work with Congress to make the immigration laws "consistent with the public safety concerns that we now have in the 21st century", instead of trying to strip the citizens of their Constitutional protections. William Pitt said in 1783, **"Necessity is the plea for every infringement of human freedom. It is argument of tyrants. It is the creed of slaves."**

I , for one, do not want the current "safety concerns" to determine to extent of my Constitutional rights. Benjamin Franklin warned that **"Any people that would give up liberty for a little temporary safety deserves neither liberty nor safety." In order to protect our liberty we must not be distracted by each new crisis. We must focus on being vigilant and looking for the real questions in the crisis; the question of narrowing our Constitutional rights is not even necessary when we open our eyes to the 800lb gorilla standing in the room with Mr. Shahzad and Mr. Holder.**

Stamp Act Ressurected

By KrisAnne Hall
www.krisannehall.com

At a recent forum Dennis Prager said, "we have forgotten what it means to be Americans". We have been sorely negligent in teaching our children about our founding fathers and the tyranny they overcame. We have failed to teach our children the Declaration of Independence, the Constitution and the principle of Natural Law which teaches us that our rights are gifted to us by our Creator and not the government. This negligence has been perpetrated for so long that we have entire generations that have no clue what tyranny looks like, or why it is important to fight for the rights we all hold by the very nature of our birth. This ignorance has permitted citizen and leader alike to sit idly by as many fundamental principles of our Republic are attacked.

George Santayana, philosopher and poet declared, "Those who do not learn from history are doomed to repeat it". Yet, here we are today, seemingly doomed to repeat the history that separated our people from the tyrannical rule of a British King.

Many today do not know that our colonists did not come to the American Continent to build a new nation; rather, they came to expand Great Britain. They sought to establish a part of the Empire in which they could freely and fully exercise their natural rights as British citizens. Our forefathers were, in fact, proud British Citizens; as late as 1765 children in the street were chanting, "King,

Pitt, and Liberty."[1] This simple chant reflected their love of the King. However, when their King's actions violated the both the Bill of Rights of 1689 and the principle of Natural Law, no love of King could sustain the colonists allegiance to a tyrant.

Few Americans understand how the Tax Acts of the 1770s drove our forefathers to demand separation from their beloved country of Great Britain. American colonists were becoming increasingly annoyed at the actions of Parliament and the fact that they had no direct representation. Since coming to the American Continent they had become accustomed to electing their officials and the direct representation guaranteed them through the Bill of Rights. So when Parliament, in 1765 passed the Stamp Act, as a measure to collect taxes to pay for the cost of the safety and security of the new Colony, the gauntlet was thrown.

The Stamp Act required that the King's stamp be purchased and placed on all printed material, ranging from legal documents to playing cards and dice. The Colonists were outraged by this direct taxation and limitation on their free speech. Up to this time the colonists voted in their own taxes when a request for funding came from the British Government. Additionally, the idea that each document must have the stamp of the government was offensive to a people who believed that it was their Creator that granted them this right and that it was not proper for the government to invoke such limitations. As if these violations were not enough, the Act also dictated that those in violation would not be

---

[1] William J. Bennett, *America, The Last Best Hope,* Nelson Current, 2006, p. 67.

tried by a jury of their peers in the colony, but would be sent to foreign soil for trial. The colonists knew that the Stamp Act was a direct violation of their rights as British Citizens, according to well established English Law and Natural Law, and the Virginia House of Burgesses quickly adopted the Virginia Resolves declaring the Act unconstitutional. The colonists intensely resisted the Stamp Act. Americans petitioned the King and Parliament, rioted, and smuggled or boycotted goods and threatened the lives of those appointed to enforce the Act. In less than a year, Parliament repealed the Stamp Act.[2]

The news of the repeal of the Stamp Act caused a resurgence of British Patriotism. New York City put up a statue of King George in honor of this repeal. The excitement of the people was so overwhelming that the people took no notice when, on the heels of the repeal of the Stamp Act, Parliament passed the Declaratory Act. This Act gave Parliament the right "to have, full power and authority to make laws and statutes of sufficient force and validity to bind the colonies and people of *America,* subjects of the crown of *Great Britain,* in all cases whatsoever".

As a result of the Declaratory Act, the Parliament began issuing a series of laws against the Colonies and because Parliament had declared them to be "fit for the good of the empire", the colonists could do nothing to challenge them. Parliament had not repealed the Stamp Act because they understood the Act to be unconstitutional,

---

[2] See Also, Andrew M. Allison, Jay A. Perry, and W. Cleon Skousen, *The Real George Washington,* National Center for Constitutional Studies, 2009.

162

they repealed it to appease and distract the people, and so they could learn and modify the Act to gain full power and authority over the colonies, "in all cases whatsoever".

Parliament had learned their lesson from the Stamp Act. They now understood that the colonists would be directly opposed to an internal tax on goods. Parliament then modified their direction to tax only items imported into the colonies and then limited the ability of the colonists to produce their own goods. The new vehicle for their methods was the Townshend Act; a taxation on glass, paint, oil, lead, paper, and tea. The Empire had also learned from the Stamp Act, that they could not employ local people to enforce these taxes and instead sent a swarm of English Custom Agents to collect these taxes and prevent smuggling. In order to enforce this Act Parliament gave the Agents of the Crown the authority to issue Writs of Assistance.

Writs of Assistance were general warrants that would be written and issued by the British Agents without judge, magistrate, or approval through a hearing. James Otis, an attorney, called these Writs of Assistance, "the worst instrument of arbitrary power, the most destructive of English liberty and the fundamental principles of law, that ever was found in an English law-book". They were literally hand written warrants that required no probable cause and little more than mere suspicion. These British Agents, often described as overzealous and corrupt, had the power to break into ships, warehouses, businesses and private homes on nothing more than a whim. Colonist vehemently opposed these clear violations of the Bill of Rights and English Law. John Dickinson, in his Letters From a Farmer, reasoned that:

In fact, if the people of New York cannot be legally taxed, but by their own representatives, they cannot be legally deprived of the privileges of making laws, only for insisting on that exclusive privilege of taxation. If they may be legally deprived, in such a case, of the privilege of making laws, why may they not, with equal reason, be deprived of every other privilege? Or what signifies the repeal of the Stamp Act, if these colonies are to lose their other privileges, by not tamely surrendering that of taxation?

The many parallels to the present day are frightening. In the wake of the McCAin-Fiengold Bill, it would not be surprising to wake up one morning to the "New Stamp Act." The machinations to find new ways to tax the people harkens back to the many Tax Acts of the 1770s and we can most certainly see paralellels to "the worst instrument of arbitrary power;" consider the Patriot Act. The underlying rationale by Parliament for the Stamp and Townshend Acts as enforced by the Writs of Assistance was the safety and security of the nation. This is how the history meets the present day. In the name of national security and safety, Congress has granted the Federal Bureau of Investigation a modern day Writ of Assistance via the <u>National Security Letters</u>.

The statute within the Patriot Act that allows for National Security Letters permits law enforcement to obtain records of people not suspected of any wrongdoing and without judge, magistrate, or court order, based upon mere suspicion. To compound the constitutional imposition of this act, those served with these letters are gagged and prohibited from disclosing that they have even been served with the threat of federal prosecution.

As you ask yourself, can this be possible, I will tell you not only is it possible, but we have already seen the tyranny of this power.

In July 2005, the FBI issued a national security letter to four Connecticut librarians. The letter sought computer subscriber data for a 45-minute period, during which a terrorist threat was *thought* to have been transmitted. In accordance to this letter, a gag order prevented the librarians from talking about the letter to anyone. The librarians refused to comply with the FBI's request. The Librarians were arrested and federally prosecuted. Federal prosecutors eventually dropped the charges, but not until these librarians were indicted and brought before a federal judge under violations of the Patriot Act.

In 2008 the Office of the Inspector General conducted an audit of the issuance of National Security Letters. The 2008 audit confirmed that the FBI increasingly used National Security Letters to seek information on U.S. citizens. From 2003 to 2006, almost 200,000 NSL requests were issued. In 2006 alone, almost 60% of the 49,425 requests were issued specifically for investigations of U.S. citizens or legal aliens. Are we to understand that our government believes that 60% of the terrorist threat in this nation comes from our own citizens? That, to me, is an ignorant supposition when we look at the fact that our own Department of Justice is refusing to prosecute prominent Muslim leaders for helping support the Hamas terrorist organization, out of fear of inflaming the American Muslim community.

As a result of several law suits initiated by the ACLU, the provisions of the Patriot Act have been altered, however these alterations were nothing more than an attempt to appease and distract the public. Provisions inserted to protect libraries were counteracted by a loophole that authorized the original power of the National Security Letters if the library contained public internet access. Provisions inserted to allow for challenge of the Letters are circumvented in the event the government declares that allowing the challenge would "harm national security". On the government's word the court must accept that assertion as "conclusive" and dismiss the challenge. Even more alarming is the fact that in February of 2010 Congress decided to reauthorize the Patriot Act for three more years.

We must also remember that in 2007, by a vote of 404 to 6, the house passed HR 1955 the Violent Radicalization and Homegrown Terrorism Act. Full passage of this Act would open the door for citizens to be prosecuted not only for actions they had taken but also for associating with certain groups or possessing certain belief systems. Just as the Townshend and Quartering Acts were stacked together and enforced by Writs of Assistance, how can the Patriot Act and the mutable definition of terrorist provided in HR 1955 combine to make an even more destructive end? Let me remind you of the observation of that Pennsylvania Farmer, "If the [rights of the people] may be legally deprived, in such a case..., why may they not, with equal reason, be deprived of every other privilege?

We have ignored the important history surrounding the Revolution of our nation and in doing so, we have allowed our own Congress to repeat its tyranny. In the name of safety and security our Constitution is being shredded, our liberties are being taken, our children's future is being destroyed. We have ignored Benjamin

Franklin's warning that those who would trade their liberties for security deserve neither liberty nor security. It appears to me that only the people of this nation are ignorant of its history. The enemies of liberty seem to be well educated and have learned from its failings and have modified tyranny accordingly. Today's challenge: Who will stand for the safety and security of OUR Constitution?

Made in the USA
Charleston, SC
30 April 2014